REACH YOUR DREAMS

REACH YOUR DREAMS

FIVE STEPS TO BE A CONSCIOUS CREATOR IN YOUR LIFE

Alice Chan, Ph.D.

Copyright © 2022 by Alice P. Chan.

ISBN 978-1-959071-59-4 (paperback)

All rights reserved. No part of this book may be reproduced or transmitted in any form or by any means, electronic or mechanical, including photocopying, recording, or by any information storage and retrieval system without express written permission from the author, except in the case of brief quotations embodied in critical reviews and certain other noncommercial uses permitted by copyright law.

Printed in the United States of America.

To all who desire to REACH your dreams

"Once you make a decision, the universe conspires to make it happen."

— Ralph Waldo Emerson

TABLE OF CONTENTS

A Ten-Year Anniversary Update 9
Prologue 17

Chapter 1: Introduction 27
Chapter 2: Release 51
Chapter 3: Envision 91
Chapter 4: Act 120
Chapter 5: Celebrate 150
Chapter 6: Honor 174
Chapter 7: Conclusion 199

Epilogue 209
Appendix: My Experience with EFT 222
Bibliography 225
Resources 227
Acknowledgements 228

A TEN-YEAR ANNIVERSARY UPDATE

This book was originally published in 2011. The content is as relevant today as it was a decade ago. If anything, in the ensuing ten years, more scientific research has been conducted with the effect of lending further credence to the consciousness principles behind the REACH program in this book.

Below, I will get into the highlights of this more recent research in this ten-year anniversary update note. But first, let me share what I have learned about REACH in this past decade.

On a morning in early July 2021, I got an intuitive hit that this book needs to circulate again, that people needed the REACH program during these trying times. As if for additional measure to minimize my dismissing this intuitive hit, I also heard from a literary agent about getting this book out.

There was no mistaking that I need to get this book circulating again. However, it still came as a huge surprise to me on multiple levels – and, quite honestly, at an inconvenient time.

First, I had just kicked into high gear to begin building my executive coaching practice. At the same time, I was also supposed to write a volume of poetry in short order. In other words, my plate was more than full. Where would I find the time to circulate a book to which I have not paid attention for eight years?

Beyond time availability, I had frankly put this book away as something I had done a long time ago. It belongs in the past. Why was I being asked to "resurrect" it after so many years? Why now?

Furthermore, in my mind, I was guided to write this book ten years ago with the general population in mind, not specifically the senior female executives I was most recently called to serve. My initial reaction was that dealing with this book would be a major distraction.

But, as I have been reminded time and again, there is a higher wisdom and intelligence that knows what my limited human mind does not, at least not until later – in some cases, much later. When that happens, it is for my own good to not know until it is time to know, as my rational mind may think it knows better and mess the whole thing up.

You will read more in this book about the criticality of tuning into and trusting a greater wisdom to guide you. That wisdom and intelligence is infinitely more powerful than your mortal mind, no matter how smart you are – trust me on this one. It will guide you to your best life being your best self – if you will get out of your own way and let it.

But I am getting ahead of myself a bit here. For now, let me just say that I have learned when I receive repeated nudges to do something, I do it, even—especially—if it does not make any logical sense. Once you read this book, you will understand why. And that applies to you as well, i.e., acting on what you feel repeatedly nudged to do, even if it does not make any sense right now.

So, you now hold in your hands a just-in-time revival of timeless principles I was guided to put into words a decade ago. The "just-in-time" part is both for your and my benefit. Allow me to elaborate a little bit in this ten-year update opening.

REACH is Based on Timeless Principles

Since the publication of this book, my spiritual practice has deepened and my faith in a Higher Power strengthened. The principles of REACH have been key foundation blocks. They are as relevant today as they were a decade ago.

As you will read in the coming pages, REACH is a program that empowers you to create the life you want, rather than having life happen to you without your say.

REACH is an acronym representing these five timeless principles:

- *Release* limiting beliefs blocking our dreams
- *Envision* living our dreams
- *Act* on divine inspiration and guidance
- *Celebrate* life for more reasons to celebrate
- *Honor* who we are as powerful creators and where we are

Each of these principles played out repeatedly during the past ten years as I continued to learn and grow as a conscious creator of my life. Let me take you through the utility of these timeless principles in turn.

To start with release, I continue to work on peeling away deeper layers of limiting beliefs. As you will read in the Release Chapter, it has taken a lifetime for each of us to register—often unknowingly—beliefs that have the effect of telling us our dreams are unrealistic and unachievable. Sometimes, they even make us question whether we deserve what we desire. Unraveling the many layers of limiting beliefs takes time and can only be done layer by layer. So, release is not a one-and-done endeavor, but a committed lifelong practice.

As for envisioning, I still vision and visualize my best life on a regular basis. Especially when life as we knew it precipitously came to a halt in the spring of 2020 because of COVID-19, I spent a lot of my free time envisioning the life I wanted to build post-pandemic. I did not want all the suffering and sacrifices, however temporary, to be for naught. I do not believe in being a powerless victim of circumstances. While there are many things in life over which I have no control, there is a lot I can shape with powerful intentions and actions.

Speaking of taking intentional actions, it is literally a way of life for me. Each morning starts with journaling and meditation to guide me on what to do. This year, I added a few simple yoga poses along with prayer to embody love in how I start my day. I literally ask to be filled up with love to give it all away in service. Then, using SMART action planning, I keep track of my goals and action plans to achieve them.

Onto celebration, its importance has especially been highlighted by the pandemic. Life is precious not to be taken for granted. We simply cannot wait for "big" reasons to celebrate. Even before the pandemic, I had made a point of celebrating little things in life to remember how much there is every day to appreciate and for which to be grateful.

Last but most certainly not least, honoring myself and where I am in my journey continues to be the biggest on-going lesson for me. Therefore, this just-in-time revival of REACH is as much for my benefit as yours.

You see, I went back to the corporate world eight years ago. During most of those years, I judged myself for "selling out." To my ego, this professional move was tantamount to my failing REACH. That was also why I wrote off this book as a piece of my past, as I could not reconcile it with my life as a corporate executive.

That was until I was guided to prepare this book for circulation again. When I re-read the Honor Chapter, it made me realize that I was called back to the corporate world for certain events to transpire—some especially difficult, as growth often entails—for me to receive my updated mission in life: To do my part to make this world safer for women, starting with the workplace.

Therefore, I am actively building an executive coaching practice. It is my reason to be to help female executives lead with their whole selves, not just their well-developed masculine side that is responsible for meticulous planning, rigorous analysis, and flawless execution.

We live in a pivotal time of change now to invite more inclusion and empathy, more heart and soul—the domain of our feminine side—not just smarts. We need our integrated, full selves to begin healing unprecedented divisions stemming from fear-based ignorance expressed as hate and fanaticism, to begin eradicating long-standing structural oppression of minority, marginalized groups.

I want to do my part to support women in power to raise consciousness in the wealth-generating sectors of society that hold the masses' livelihood in the hands of those in their leadership ranks, especially the upper echelons. I hope to recruit evolved powerful male allies to join in this consciousness crusade, to end unconscious perpetuation of outdated fear-based structures, systems and norms that continue to exclude, oppress, and abuse.

So, a huge reason for me being told to circulate this book again is for me to recognize my judgment of my eight-year "detour"—and honor this segment of my journey. I truly could not have come to my current realization of my role at this juncture in human history without this critical segment of my journey.

Connection Between Neuroscience and Spirituality

Our logical mind seeks proof. Existing in a five-sensory world leads us to buy into the belief that only what we can see, hear, touch, taste and/or feel is real. That is what science does for those of us who believe we are no more than mere mortals – to furnish proof for the existence of something, to make it ok to believe it to be real.

REACH is premised on believing into existence that which we want to experience. Don't get me wrong, there are lots of things beyond our control. However, we are not completely at the mercy of external circumstances either. Life does not just happen *to* us. There is a lot we can do to shape it, along with our response to what we cannot control, such that life happens *for* us.

That said, REACH is not simply perpetuating new-age woo-woo. In the coming chapters, you will read about some of the scientific basis for belief preceding experience. This includes the works of Dr. Bruce Lipton on the biology of belief and Dr. Deepak Chopra on intuitive intelligence. These were cited in the original 2011 printing, which I have preserved in this ten-year anniversary edition.

In the decade since the original publication of this book, there has been more neuroscience research evidence supporting the notion that we can actively shape our experiences. Practices like gratitude journaling and meditation I advocate in REACH have been shown to have the effect of rewiring our brain. This goes beyond positive thinking to having tangible improved outcomes in our lives.

For instance, more research in neuroplasticity shows that meditation has the effect of lowering stress and anxiety levels. You may have heard of the evolutionary adaptive responses triggered in our amygdala of fight, flight, or freeze when we perceive our safety being threatened. That is, we either fight the threat, run as fast as we can, or freeze/play dead. The freeze response is arguably less likely to be useful in modern day emotional safety challenges vs. what our ancestors faced in the wild with life-or-death threats.

Besides instructing us to fight, run, or freeze in the face of a perceived threat, it turns out that our amygdala can also produce a "tend-and-befriend" response. By cultivating social connections to extend caring and to seek support when threatened, we build resilience and cultivate courage. From an evolutionary standpoint, we are more likely to survive a threat in larger numbers with our tribe than alone.

These newer insights come from research in the biology of courage. For an accessible and informative discussion on this subject, you may want to look up a Ted Talk, "How to Make Stress Your Friend," by Dr. Kelly McGonigal. In this presentation, she shares research on how an altered view of stress changes our physiological response and helps us turn stress into a helpful ally.

Specifically, our heart may automatically pound in the face of stress no matter how we view stress. However, if we see stress as preparation for rising to a challenge instead of being something harmful, our blood vessels will stay relaxed – as if we are in states of joy and courage. In other words, it is not a given that stress can kill us. It is the *belief* in its harm that could do actual harm. More importantly, that belief can be changed into a life-affirming one.

Besides rewiring our brain to view stress as an ally, we can further fortify our ability to face perceived threats by building a tribe around us. By seeking to be surrounded by those with whom we share mutual caring, we show ourselves that we can handle challenges – and we do not have to do it alone.

Daring to dream and attempting to realize it requires us to venture out of our comfort zone and face the unknown. It is all but guaranteed to trigger fear and stress. As you will see in the coming chapters in this book, there are spiritual and consciousness-raising practices you can cultivate to achieve scientifically observed benefits of building resilience and rising to challenges effectively.

By building our courage, resilience, and social support, we have a higher chance of sticking through the scary spots and not giving up too soon or sabotaging our progress, whether knowingly or unknowingly. After all, being courageous does not mean we never feel fear. It is doing what scares us anyway.

Supporting You to REACH Your Dreams

As you will see in the coming pages, REACH is a step-by-step program with contemplation exercises. To support you to REACH your dreams, I have created a companion workbook that you can download

Alice P. Chan, Ph.D.

for free at dralicechan.com. It is my gift to you to help you maximize your chances of reaping the benefits of working this program.

Whether you download the workbook or use your own journal or notebook, I cannot stress enough how important it is for you to do the exercises. Just reading the book will not give you the results you want.

Without further ado, I invite you to begin your REACH journey. I feel the same today what I felt ten years ago when I wrote this book – it is an honor and a privilege of a lifetime to be guided to share a program with you that empowers you to create the life of your dreams.

I wish you all kinds of happiness, success, abundance, and fulfillment.

With Love and Blessings,

PROLOGUE

Finish REACH book. Just do it. You have a message to share. Don't delay.

The above was one of the messages I got on New Year's Eve 2010, when I sat down to review the year and to prepare for 2011. I wanted to close out 2010 with gratitude for all the people and events that graced my life during the last year. I also wanted to release any lingering negative feelings or latent old beliefs that no longer served me.

To prepare for 2011, I contemplated intentions I wanted to set for the New Year, and led myself through a couple of my favorite meditations. In very clear and direct terms, finishing this book emerged as a top priority coming from deep within – the wisest and most creative part of me, which is connected to the all-knowing, all-powerful, all-loving source energy.

Among other messages I received, two of them have become my guiding principles for 2011: *Become the best version of you. Love awaits harvesting in your heart.*

As I am writing the book you now hold in your hands, I tell myself to step into the best version of me – and own it – and to speak to you with the love of life that is overflowing from my heart.

The Story of REACH

The idea of this book first came to me in March 2008, when I was visiting Sedona, a place renowned for its natural beauty and spiritual vortices. I went there at the invitation of a friend who told me that sitting on Bell Rock would set change in motion – whether or not I was ready for it. Even though I was not sure I believed that, I was most certainly up for change. More importantly, I was open to receiving *any* guidance on what to do next with my restless and discontented life.

You see, for as long as I could remember, I had been wondering for what purpose I came into this life. By the Sedona trip, I was really feeling the emotional wear-and-tear of having spent years searching – seemingly in vain – for the answer. It felt like I had worn out my buffer, and if I had to tolerate another day of just marking time in this life, I would burst! I desperately needed to figure out why I was born, what I was meant to be, and what I was meant to do in this life.

Over the years of searching for my soul's purpose, I was exposed to many great thoughts, profound teachings and eye-opening tools about how I could be a *conscious creator* of my own life. It was up to me to cultivate a consciousness of how I manifest experiences, instead of continuing to wonder why things *happened to* me.

By my visit to Sedona, not only was I wrestling with the great discomfort of my existential crisis, I was also experiencing major information overload. I had not fully sorted out, integrated or assimilated the vast array of self-help tools and personal development teachings I had picked up. More than anything in the world, my overwhelmed self wished someone had just handed me a clearly laid out roadmap, an integrated process with just the right tools to guide me through resolving my crisis and revealing my soul's purpose.

While in Sedona, I had an epiphany. I could not possibly be the only person on Planet Earth experiencing these struggles. I must have signed up for my life experiences so that I could learn what I needed to learn in order to serve those on a similar path – the kindred souls who also wondered similarly what they were doing in their human body suits and how they, too, could become conscious creators in their own lives. I imagined there must be so many like-minded others, lost and wondering where to begin to find their way, equally overwhelmed by all the self-help tools available. They, too, must wish there was a clear roadmap to guide them on their path to greater purpose and happiness.

I thought to myself: What if *I* were to develop such a roadmap, such a process to help guide those who were tired of being victims of circumstances, but instead wished to manifest the life of their dreams? What if it was *my* calling to develop and share a personal empowerment process that would resonate with those who wrestled with similar unrest and frustration? What if it was *my* life purpose to be a living proof that, yes, there *is* an easier, better and more fulfilling way to live – and here is how?

Nearly as soon as I had the above epiphany, the name for the process, REACH, came to me as effortlessly and quickly as if via a direct high-speed connection to cosmic wisdom. REACH was to be an acronym for the personal empowerment roadmap I would create: *Release, Envision, Act, Celebrate* and *Honor*. These process steps would integrate what I had learned from all the personal development resources to which I was exposed. Backed by my own experience with following this roadmap, I would be able to serve others in a very personally meaningful way.

I immediately pictured a book and workshops to teach this process. I felt more alive than I had in a long time. I was over the moon with excitement. With the prospect of helping to transform and empower lives through REACH, at long last, I had found my elusive life purpose!

Filled with so much enthusiasm and energy, why wasn't this book published in 2008, or even in 2009? Why didn't I finish it until 2011?

Alice P. Chan, Ph.D.

My Barriers to REACH

To be perfectly candid, I simply chickened out – not just once, but again and again. When I first sat down to write this book in 2008, after returning home from Sedona, I was really excited about the concept of REACH. I saw glimpses of how bringing this work to life would fulfill my life purpose, and could imagine vividly helping innumerable others transform their lives.

Unfortunately, I was even more filled with fears and self-doubt, which over-powered any enthusiasm or passion I felt at the time for bringing this work to life. With the clarity of hindsight, I did not believe in myself sufficiently then to be able to communicate clearly and authentically the life-altering message of this book.

I was paralyzed by the terror of failing. What if nobody wanted to read this book? What if I fell flat on my face venturing into the area of personal empowerment in which I did not have much of a professional track record? How would I ever be able to make a living doing this?

Even though I had hungered for more meaning in my professional life, in how I made a living, I was objectively very good at what I did as a market research and business consultant. Besides, in that profession, I was able to put my many years of formal education to good use, after leaving my academic career behind at the start of the millennium. It was simply not that easy to walk away from conscious competence. I was really attached to the intellectual and emotional investments I had made in my professional life, and was not ready to let them all go to waste.

Aside from the fear of failing, I was also afraid of leaving my comfort zone. Yes, I was quite bitter about being over-worked and under-paid for years, and extremely frustrated that my career was stagnating. However, my job was my comfort zone. Even though I was grossly unhappy in my comfort zone, my professional misery was predictable and, more importantly, controllable to me.

My fearful self thought I would be safer in my known misery than in the uncertainty of venturing into the unknown of a new career. I was gripped by the fear of not being able to survive and keep myself safe if I left my job and pursued REACH. I was inadvertently waiting for a guarantee that this risk was worth taking. Of course, that guarantee never came. Life does not offer guarantees.

Although my fears were big and paralyzing, I must be honest and say that fears alone wouldn't have stopped me cold in my tracks. After all, I knew I had enough determination, tenacity and perseverance to do anything I truly wanted. If I believed in this book enough, I would have kept my day job and scraped together the hours needed to write until it was published. There was no need to give up my comfort zone entirely before I was ready for the complete leap.

Truthfully, the bigger barrier was the immense self-doubt overshadowing any passion or conviction I felt for this project. This self-doubt added fuel to the fire of my fears about financial – and, ultimately, emotional – security. Quite simply, I did not feel qualified to write a book like this or teach personal empowerment. Who did I think I was anyway? Why would anyone want to listen to a woman whom they have never heard of? As much I was really passionate about the idea of REACH, I had yet to believe that *I* could do something like this. To the inner critic within me, I had not *earned* the credibility to do this.

While I am being very honest with you here, I was not always quite so honest about doubting myself. Instead, I would come up with a million and one *legitimate* reasons why I could not finish this book. *I'm too busy working to make a living, especially in a tough economy. The timing isn't right, yet. I'm too weak physically* (you will find out why in a moment). *I have just become self-employed, and don't have the time or energy to write.*

Alice P. Chan, Ph.D.

On and on the excuses went. Anyway, you get the idea. This self-doubt ended up stopping me a few times over the last three years when I attempted to get back to this book project and finish it.

The Life-Altering Blessing

The pivotal event that eventually got me past my fears and self-doubt was a near-death experience on December 30, 2008. I was in a car accident in which I sustained severe head trauma. To this day, I have no memory of what exactly happened that got me rushed to Stanford Hospital, unconscious, bleeding internally and externally in my head. Let's just say that I am very fortunate to be alive and thriving today.

This objectively traumatic event is a blessing to me because, while I was in the hospital, I experienced something that will always remind me of who I really am and from where I came.

It was a very special moment of feeling the Presence, of being wrapped up, protected and held by Divine Love. At one point, while lying unconscious in the Intensive Care Unit, long before I was aware of how badly injured I was, I sensed a very bright light. Then, a clear knowing came upon me: *I almost died.*

With that knowing came the realization that, since I was kept alive, there must be more for me to do in this life. I immediately felt a very strong, unwavering sense of conviction that I must find out what that is and do it! I had never felt so sure about anything in my life.

Along with this knowing, I became aware of a tremendous amount of love enveloping my entire being, like the most comforting, protective, warm blanket. My heart and my entire being were so cradled by this love that felt much bigger and more powerful than anything I had ever experienced. It was the most loved I had felt in my entire life, and I was filled with a profound sense of peace and security. I felt that all was well and exactly in the right order. This is despite the fact that, at the time, there was a trauma team of six surgeons working to keep me alive. And, I was physically connected to all kinds of advanced medical devices to stabilize and monitor my condition. I woke up three days later with staples running across the top and down to the side of my head, and a huge open wound with raw flesh exposed in the left side of my forehead. You could say that my near-death experience gave me the gumption and the conviction to go after the life I am meant to live. That is, once I regained my strength.

As profound as that experience was, I was challenged by the recovery. It took months to heal physically from the severe trauma to the head. In addition to the physical challenges, I struggled with post-traumatic stress, and went through a period of intense fear and loneliness that felt like an eternity. That was until I woke up one day and decided that I was sick and tired of merely surviving. I was ready to thrive again. With that clear intention set, within a couple of months, I started feeling better and getting stronger.

Once I lifted myself out of survival mode, I started taking stock of my life leading up to the dramatic wakeup call of the accident. Afraid or not, doubtful of my credibility or not, I did not get a second lease on life to continue marking time in an unsatisfying existence. It was time to leave my comfort zone – but in a way that I was ready and able to do at the time.

I knew it was too big of a leap to go from a profession I knew well to a completely different line of work *and* to become self-employed all at the same time. So, I left my job to be an independent business consultant. I felt that this intermediate step would give me a chance to detach fully from the security I had attributed to being employed by someone else, in preparation for being self-employed in a completely different field. Effectively, I honored where I was on my life path at that time and the extent to which I was ready to stretch myself then.

Alice P. Chan, Ph.D.

The Integration

All in all, it would take another two years after the accident before I was truly ready to finish this book – to live and learn more, and to cultivate the courage and humility to be honest with myself. As even the most prolific authors will tell you, we learn as we process deeply what we want to write, just as good teachers will tell you that we teach what we most want to practice ourselves.

I finally realized that writing this book does not require me to be a fool-proof expert on life who knows it all. Instead, what qualifies me to write this book is that it is my own journey of awakening to my soul's purpose for being here in this life. I already have all the credibility in the world to write what no one else can convey as well as I can – my very own experiences of practicing conscious living to REACH my dreams, to fulfill my life purpose. And, it is with a deep desire for you to REACH yours that I share with you this work of love from my heart and soul.

In choosing to disclose to you my less than glamorous, stop-and-go experience of birthing this book, I am hoping that my struggle with fears and self-doubt would resonate with you at some level. More importantly, it is my genuine desire that you recognize – just as I did over the years – that it is important to honor the lessons your fearful, doubtful moments teach you.

Cliché as it may sound, mine taught me a lot, and strengthened my resolve to rise above them. Moreover, if you believe strongly enough in your dreams, no fear or doubt can permanently take you off course. Your life purpose simply will not leave you alone until you step into it and own it.

Therefore, there is no need to fret too much about *not yet* being clear about your dreams, or judge yourself too harshly for *not yet* having gotten your act together to go after them. Uncomfortable as it feels now, you *cannot* miss your life. Just be willing to look more and more to the wisest and most fearless part of yourself for a little more courage each time the call to follow your path comes knocking on your door.

As you listen more and more to the guidance of your inner voice, the beautiful picture of your dream life will unfold before you. And, if you are willing, the REACH process in this book is intended to help you reveal this picture and make it a reality.

In the years it took to bring this book to life, I reflected on where I had been in my life and what I had experienced – from the most joyful memories to the most painful times. I have learned that I was always exactly where I needed to be, no matter how unpleasant or downright painful the objective circumstances were at the time.

It always made sense later why these losses and challenges were real gifts, not just the blissful moments that are naturally easy to love and appreciate. If I had lived a life free of struggles, it would never have fueled the passion and conviction I feel for writing this book, no matter how many times I felt discouraged.

Ultimately, there really *is* a good reason for everything, whether or not it feels that way to us at the moment of the most excruciating pain or the deepest despair. The important key is whether we *choose* to have the courage to accept the great gifts of the life lessons we attracted into our lives, or *choose* victimhood, hanging onto the grievance stories about the painful and unfair hand we were dealt.

It is *always* a matter of choice, no exception. We all have the privilege to make that choice over and over again in this life. I know what my choice is. What is *yours*?

As you prepare to REACH your dreams, I have one more note of encouragement to share. From my own experiences, I am here to attest to the truth that we can never fail when we listen to our inner voice for the right action.

Alice P. Chan, Ph.D.

On my path to find and live an authentic life, I left *four* highly respectable, even prestigious, jobs at different points in time without having lined up the source of my next paycheck. Yet, with each of the four leaps of faith, in the absence of a visible net to catch me, I never even came close to becoming destitute. In every case, the net appeared *after* I jumped. And, after every leap, I always landed on my feet, and ended up better off emotionally and financially.

When we act according to the integrity of who we are, following the guidance from the best and most creative version of ourselves, we simply cannot fail. With each successful leap we make, our faith in life – and in ourselves – grows, too. Mine most certainly has. As faith deepens, a tremendous sense of freedom follows.

When we believe that life is always on our side, we welcome the great joy of being liberated from fears and self-doubt. From that place of fearless creation, anything is possible, and true prosperity abounds.

So, at long last, you hold this book in your hands, a long time in coming since that faithful visit to Sedona in 2008, the birthplace of this roadmap to REACH the life of my dreams – and now, hopefully for you to REACH yours, too.

Congratulations on saying a huge "Yes!" to REACH your dreams! May your days be filled with endless moments of ease and delight. May your life of conscious choice take you to outrageous success, happiness and fulfillment beyond your wildest imagination. May your heart always, always be overflowing with love, joy, grace and peace. Let it all be so, and so it is.

With Love and Gratitude,

Alice Chan, Ph.D.
Belmont, California

CHAPTER 1

Introduction

*"Go confidently in the direction of your dreams.
Live the life you have imagined."*

— Henry David Thoreau

The above quote has been my inspiration for many years. These two simple sentences perfectly capture the passion and conviction I feel for the life I want to live – and what I am about to share with you in this book.

First, use your imagination to compose the life of your dreams. Then, with unwavering confidence about the life you have imagined, allow it to lead you into action. After all, everything big and small begins as simple figments of imagination on the part of the inspired souls who go confidently in the direction of their dreams.

Technological advances and modern-day conveniences all materialize for our edification because, at some point, someone dared to imagine. And, they believed in their dreams so much that not only did they themselves take action, but they were able to mobilize action on the part of many others to help bring their dreams to life on a grand scale.

Quite simply, when we combine our imagination with purposeful action, we have the winning recipe for manifesting our dreams, no matter their scale.

I know, many of you are thinking that this is so much easier said than done. If it were so simple, why aren't we all living our dreams right now? Why do some of us feel so bogged down by responsibilities that we either feel that dreaming is frivolous or that we don't know how to dream?

Trust me, we all know how to dream, but we have simply forgotten. I stared at the above Thoreau quote for many years to keep myself inspired before I could actually follow the advice. Ironically, when I was a little girl, I loved to imagine things, and spent many hours daydreaming in the privacy of my own mind.

Just ask young children to imagine, and exciting worlds with lively characters are created. Since they have yet to learn to be afraid of failing or to doubt themselves, everything is possible, and the sky is the limit.

Of course, we don't have to be children to imagine, and we certainly can get excited about possibilities at any age. However, as adults, we may have to release the fears and self-doubt we have inadvertently accumulated over the course of our lives. It does not mean we never feel fear or doubt again. It just means we do not let them stop us. We may have to consciously give ourselves full permission to dream, to stay true to our heart's desires, and to take bold action to make them a reality.

Keeping Ourselves Safe vs. Dreaming

From Maslow's Hierarchy of Needs, we learn that our most basic human needs have to do with feeling physically and emotionally safe.[1]

---

[1] Presented as a pyramid, Maslow's Hierarchy of Needs places physiological needs for air, food, water, etc., at the base, on top of which is layered safety that comes from employment, family, health and other resources. Above these needs, we have love and a sense of belonging, followed by esteem for self and others. At the top of the pyramid is self-actualization. Until our basic needs are met, the desire for self-actualization would be thwarted.

When we perceive that our core needs are unmet or threatened in any way, all our physical, mental and emotional resources are instinctively directed to achieve or restore a sense of safety.

Unless we believe that we are safe at the most fundamental level, it would be challenging for higher-level desires to flourish. Until a solid foundation of security is established in our perceived reality, any inkling of a want – instead of a need – would be over-powered by our survival instincts. As a result, there would be insufficient fuel for the engine of higher-level desires, such as our dreams, and what we get are very visceral feelings of *I just can't do this*.

From my own personal experience, at the lowest points in my life, it was literally a struggle to see even a glimmer of hope, let alone dream. My creative space was totally jammed with fear, and I was completely consumed by being in survival mode. And, when I got myself sufficiently established and allowed myself to dream, I lacked the confidence to follow through with making my desires a reality.

You just read in the Prologue about my challenges in finishing this book, even though it has been a dream of mine for several years. In the end, the good news is that, once the dream was born, there was no denying it. In time, I learned to get out of my own way and surrender to the power of my dream to carry me forward. I finally allowed the calling from deep within to activate the confidence and tenacity within me – which have been there all along waiting to be harvested – to follow the call, to take inspired action to allow this dream to come true.

I want to say to you most emphatically that you, too, can make your dreams come true! I know what torture it is to feel stuck in a life that seems pointless, to feel so blocked that you don't even know what you really want, or to feel scared and powerless to go after what you love. The personal empowerment roadmap in this book – REACH – is intended to help you clear the blocks in your creative energy field, imagine living the life of your dreams, and take confident action in manifesting it.

Remove the Roadblocks and Take Action

Picture in your mind's eye a path in front of you. Where you are standing is where you are in your life right now. Somewhere ahead of you is where you want to be – when your dreams are fulfilled. You may be able to visualize what living your dreams is like, or you may not have a clue, but simply that there has got to be a better life than the one you have right now.

While you may be able to picture where you want to be, you cannot see the path ahead to get you there. Instead, from where you stand currently, what is within view may be only the roadblocks keeping you from where you want to go.

The roadblocks you see in your mind's eye are your fears, worries and self-doubt that keep you from going confidently toward where you want to go. These blocks are limiting beliefs you have about yourself that come in as many variations as there are stars in the night sky. *I'm not smart/educated/experienced enough. I'm too old/young for what I want. I have too many responsibilities at this point in my life to do anything different. Who would be interested in what I have to say/create? I honestly don't even know what I want; I just know that I don't want what I have now.* These are just some examples that may resonate.

Limiting thoughts and beliefs often disguise themselves as *legitimate* excuses as to why we are stuck where we are, why it is practically impossible to be, have or do something different, why it is not prudent to change the status quo – a.k.a. our comfort zone – even if we may be miserable in it. Limiting beliefs carry the voice of our otherwise well-meaning ego, whose noble job is to keep us safe.

Remember, fundamentally, we need to feel safe before we can do anything else. Because of that job description, our risk-adverse ego continually cautions us against venturing into the uncertainty of going after our dreams. Instead, it urges us to keep the known status quo, our comfort zone, even though we are unhappy in it.

For most of our limiting beliefs, their seeds were planted in our subconscious when we were really young, based on what we internalized from our environment – home, school, church and community. Over time, these beliefs become the subconscious programming that runs our lives without our conscious recognition.

According to Dr. Bruce Lipton, we got the most powerful and influential parts of this programming before we reach the age of six.[2] Our subconscious is the part of our brain that is in charge of responding to things in our environment that do not require conscious processing. It is a million times more powerful than our conscious, rational mind. Therefore, while our conscious mind is busy thinking about who we want to be and what we want to do when we grow up, our subconscious mind is on automatic pilot, rapidly helping us make decisions without much conscious thought.

Until we become aware of the latent self-limiting beliefs stored in our subconscious – and the life patterns they automatically generate – we will continue to perpetuate the same limiting life circumstances. But, the good news is that, we *can* retrieve the outdated tape of limiting beliefs that unknowingly runs our lives. In its place, we can install new empowering programming that reflects the truth of who we are, not what we had internalized as children that does not serve us.

As Dr. Lipton explains, just like we cannot change recorded programming on a tape by talking to it, we cannot change beliefs simply

---

[2] Dr. Bruce Lipton is the author of many works, including *The Biology of Belief*. He speaks often about the connection between spirituality and physiology. For a good introduction, read the chapter he wrote, "Revealing the Wizard Behind the Curtain," in *Measuring the Immeasurable: The Scientific Case for Spirituality*.

by thinking positively. We need to become aware of these old beliefs, and replace them with new ones, including the most critical one – that we are so very worthy of everything just as we are, not the least of which is the life of our dreams. Our very first step is to be *willing* to believe.

To give you an example, a very common limiting belief that most of us have is that we have to work really hard to make money. Does that resonate? When we have that underlying belief in our subconscious programming, our circumstances reflect that. We keep finding ourselves in jobs that require long, stressful hours. For some of us, we may carry the additional grievance story that life is not fair or that we don't deserve better. In that case, not only do we feel over-worked, we manifest a professional life in which we are under-paid and under-appreciated as well.

As a matter of fact, I had jobs with all of the above conditions for years. These conditions were mirrors reflecting back to me what I believed about myself, the world around me and the life I thought I deserved. When I retrieved that old tape of limiting beliefs, invalidated and released these messages, I cleared the path for great work-life balance, making more money while working a lot less, and being greatly appreciated for my contributions.

Aside from releasing self-sabotaging beliefs, we also need to take action in order for our dreams to come true. Simply visualizing our dreams in our minds is not enough for their manifestation. Yes, it is important to know our desires and to allow their presence in our belief system to empower us to break through fears and insecurities. But, beyond that, we need to take action.

Remember that dreams come true because the dreamers not only have a clear vision of what they want, they are able to inspire and mobilize action – their own and potentially others' – to make their dreams a reality. So, taking action is a key element in the formula for realizing our dreams.

There are different kinds of action, however, and this is a critical point. Acting out of fear that we need to control our environment to keep ourselves safe is fundamentally very different from taking expansive action that aligns with a clear purpose. Fear-based action takes care of basic survival needs at best, and cannot fulfill higher-level desires. It takes inspired action to realize our dreams.

Moreover, as a society, we have somehow adopted an unfortunate manic pace, such that we are constantly running somewhere, doing something – lots of busy action. Quiet time for contemplation and reflection is under-rated, and we feel like we would risk losing out if we took the time to think before we act. There is no time for thoughtful action, but instead we are constantly in reactive mode, playing catch-up, putting out fires. This is most certainly not the type of action that manifests dreams.

When we act out of fear and desperation, our body tenses up and our heart contracts. By contrast, when we are inspired by a dream, we can hardly wait to get to it. The feelings are of excitement and anticipation. Just pay attention to our intelligent body, and it will tell us whether our actions are inspired by our highest good or motivated by fear to keep us safe.

When we go confidently in the direction of our dreams, it calls for purposeful action that is inspired by a vision and guided by a clear intention – not frantic action aimed at controlling a situation or running away from circumstances out of fear.

What is REACH?

In a nutshell, *REACH Your Dreams* is a roadmap to empower you to release limiting beliefs, break through old patterns, and clear the path for your dreams to manifest. This roadmap also includes tools to help you get clear about what you want and to create your own guided action plan. Furthermore, we will talk about how to prepare for distractions and show-stoppers along the way, as well as the importance of celebrating milestones achieved in your action plan. Moreover, we will devote some time to talk about a very important part of your personal transformation journey – the need to honor who you are and where you are on your life path, as your dreams start from where you are right now.

Through meditations, contemplation exercises and strategic action planning, this book will walk you through how to *consciously* create the life of your dreams.

REACH is a mnemonic for *Release, Envision, Act, Celebrate* and *Honor*. In this book, one chapter is devoted to each of these five components of your personal empowerment roadmap.

First, **Release** (Chapter 2) is about letting go of limiting beliefs and subconscious programming – fears, worries, and doubts – running our lives. These messages take up room in our creative space, block our imagination, keep us playing safe and small, and zap us of the fire power to create the life of our dreams.

Some common ones are: *I'm not educated enough; I'm not smart enough; I'm too old (too young) to be successful at this; I can't make a living doing that; I can't afford to fail.* By bringing these limiting beliefs to the forefront, challenging their truth and validity, releasing them from our creative space, and reprogramming our subconscious mind with empowering beliefs, we take a critical step toward clearing the path for our dreams to come true.

Envision (Chapter 3) has to do with picturing living our dreams in which we have exactly what we want and, more importantly, *feeling* what it is like to have them already. In this chapter, we will focus on getting clear about the conditions and qualities of what we want, so that we can feed our imagination and activate its power to carry us forward.

With clarity around our desires, we can then be purposeful about manifesting our dreams, and submit a very clear request to the universe to be fulfilled – all backed by the power of our beliefs.

Act (Chapter 4) is about taking action on our dreams – not *busy* action that follows fear-based directives from the ego, but *guided* action coming from the wisest, most creative part of ourselves. We will look at how to discern true guidance from ego directives. Then, we will discuss creating an action plan that is SMART (Specific, Measurable, Actionable, Realistic, Time-trackable).

In this chapter, we will consider what might stop us from achieving each SMART goal. We want to be prepared for potential show stoppers, such that they don't sabotage our dreams prematurely.

It is critical to ***Celebrate*** (Chapter 5) our lives in general and each specific milestone we hit in acting on the SMART goals we envisioned for ourselves. Celebrating our wins and successful actions keeps us motivated and activates gratitude. It trains our subconscious to recognize the progress we are making in being a conscious creator of our destiny.

Our SMART action plan will include ways in which we will celebrate achieving each SMART goal. We will also talk about cultivating a consciousness of appreciation and gratitude, so that we can choose to live in a state of grace and welcome celebratory energy.

Last, but not least, ***Honor*** (Chapter 6) who we are currently and where we are on our path, since we create from the here and now. We will also talk about honoring our body, as well as things that are challenging to appreciate at their face value but which may bear wonderful gifts for us. They include the waiting time for dreams to manifest, distractions that show up and people we meet on our path. We will close with honoring our dreams by taking care of what is ours to do and surrendering control of the rest.

Alice P. Chan, Ph.D.

Foundational Principles

Before you embark on your REACH journey, let me tell you more about the foundational principles behind this personal empowerment roadmap.

Belief Precedes Experience

The core foundational principle of REACH is that our beliefs create our experience, not the other way around. It is based on a universal principle that *like attracts like*. We attract experiences into our lives which match our beliefs.

In *The Power of Intention*, the late Dr. Wayne Dyer taught us that we need to be a match for that which we want in our lives. If we want happiness, we need to get into a state of being magnetic to positive experiences. We cannot walk around with a perpetual dark cloud hanging over our head and expect life to magically turn around. Our reality starts with us and our beliefs. We attract what we are not what we want, also taught Dr. Dyer in *Excuses Begone!*

Our beliefs, as expressed through our thoughts and feelings, vibrate at different frequencies. The experiences we draw into our lives must match the same frequencies. That is why when we think positive thoughts that make us feel good, we attract more positive, good-feeling experiences.

Abraham-Hicks teachings use the analogy of radio broadcasting to explain this point.[3] We are like a radio receiver, in that what we get depends on the channel into which we are tuned, the frequencies with which we are aligned to receive. Our attitudes, beliefs and outlook – stored in our subconscious mind and expressed through our thoughts and feelings – set the dial on our radio tuner. If a radio is tuned into

---

3 Esther Hicks (with her late husband Jerry) has published a number of books on the teachings of Abraham. She also conducts workshops. (See www.abraham-hicks.com.)

the frequencies of a station playing classical music, that is the type of music it receives. It will not get communication between a pilot and the air traffic control tower at the airport.

By the same token, we attract people and events that mirror how we consciously and unconsciously see ourselves, our lives and the world around us. We *always* get to be right.

For instance, if our dominant belief is that life is a struggle, the circumstances of our lives will reflect that – our relationships are challenging, our work is unfulfilling and stressful, we cannot seem to get out of debt, and/or we just cannot shed those extra pounds no matter what we do.

Conversely, when we believe that life is easy and on our side, we find ourselves surrounded by loving, supportive people in our personal and professional lives, abundance abounds, and we are inspired to appreciate and take care of our physical body.

If you are new to this perspective, you may find it to be reverse logic. After all, you feel quite certain that your beliefs and outlook are shaped by your life experiences, not the other way around, right?

When I was first introduced to this perspective in 2006, I was skeptical about it myself. However, I did study in college the psychological concept of *self-fulfilling prophecies* – our mind is wired to seek evidence to fulfill our beliefs. As such, if I were to choose good-feeling thoughts, the worst that could happen was that I would feel better. That alone was appealing enough to me, whether or not I would end up transforming my life.

As I began to shift my focus, I started noticing changes in other people's behavior in response to mine. In time, as I continued to increase my consciousness, the drama and unnecessary strife – and the associated people – that used to be my companions gradually fell away.

It became increasingly clear to me that this perspective empowers me to be the creator of my own destiny. It is a much better way to live than to continue wondering why things happen to me. At this point, my life is mostly peaceful, joyful and grace-filled, and I rarely draw in negative experiences. When I do find myself with something unpleasant, I always know why and, more importantly, how to shift my consciousness to usher it out of my life.

If you still want further proof points, let's find something from your own experience, shall we? Take a moment and think of a time when you got something you were told you could not have. What happened there? Your desire and belief got you what you wanted without a doubt, overpowering any limiting message you received, didn't it? And, the circumstances did line up in your favor, instead of those consistent with the opposing message, right?

Contemplate other proof points in your own experience or that of others close to you. When you really want something – when you feel the fire burning in your belly, and every fiber of your being feels that it is inevitable that you have it – the universe conspires to deliver that to you. By law, the external circumstances of your life must line up to match your internal state.

If you say you want something, and yet you walk around with contrary beliefs, whether or not you are aware of that dissonance, you are effectively daring the universe to prove you wrong. It simply does not work that way. You *always* get to be right.

Therefore, if you want, say, a loving partnership, you need to uncover and release any contradictory attitudes or worries you may be holding in your vibrational offering, such as: *Truly good matches for me are rare; It is very difficult for me to find someone who truly understands me; I'm too old/fat/unattractive to be lovable.* If you broadcast any thoughts and feelings along these lines, even unconsciously, you get to be right, and you will not get that romantic partnership you desire. These subconscious messages are literally blocking your path to the partner of your dreams.

Practice changing your broadcast signals into empowering ones, such as: *I see it all the time that there is someone perfect for everyone of all different shapes, sizes, ages and objective attractiveness; I have the perfect combination of qualities that is an exact match for the desires of my life partner; Everything I have experienced puts me right on the path to meet my soulmate.*

As outlined above, the different chapters will take you through different tools to align your beliefs with your dreams and to take guided, inspired action to realize them. This process is meant to help you be the woman/man for whom you want to be loved, the colleague for whom you want to be valued, the best caregiver to your heart, mind, body and soul you could manifest.

REACH is Non-linear

For those of us who live in the United States, we live in a culture that favors logical thinking in linear terms. You know, take one step in front of another in a straight line until you get from Point A to Point B. Taking a step back would be tantamount to failing, and taking a step sideways would mean veering off your path, being distracted, undisciplined and unfocused.

However, life is non-linear. It is more like a mysterious labyrinth. Pause and think about that for a moment. If you have ever traced a labyrinth, you know that it is anything but a straight line between the start and end points. Instead, the path is wrapped around multiple folds, winding around a full circle, before reaching the goal in the center. More than a few times, it looks as if you are almost there, only to find that the path leads you away from it. Other times, it seems like you are nowhere near the center, have overshot it, or have even gone backwards. But, as long as you trust the path and keep following it, eventually you do reach the center goal.

REACH honors the labyrinth of life, and is a cyclical, non-linear process. That is, any one of the five steps in the roadmap can be the focus at any point in your own journey to realize your dreams. Any component can be repeated as many times as necessary. Especially after you have gone through the process once and know all the five elements, you can jump from any one of them to any other as needed.

For instance, if your circumstances are far from ideal, being steeped in fear and feeling trapped can really block your creative flow. Remember that we need to feel safe before higher-level desires can flourish. If you find it challenging to envision your desires, it may be valuable to examine what blocks need to be released by going back to some of the exercises in the *Release* chapter.

Similarly, if you experience difficulty coming up with realistic actions for a dream, you may want to go back to the tools in the *Envision* chapter to get more guidance on your next steps. Still another example is that you may find self-judgment creeping up and potentially derailing you. In that case, you may be comforted by jumping ahead to reading parts of the *Honor* chapter.

REACH is designed to flex with your particular situation and where you are on your path at any moment. You can use the process over and over again, in part or in whole, and in any order until you realize your dreams – and to create new ones!

REACH Uses a Balanced Approach

This personal empowerment roadmap of REACH leverages the light or healthy side of both our masculine and feminine energies. You may have heard of Yin and Yang. Regardless of your sex, you have both feminine (Yin) and masculine (Yang) energies at your disposal.

Masculine or Yang energy is associated with rational, logical thinking. It is directive, outwardly focused and firm. You run your masculine energy to define goals and objectives, chart the course to plan and get things done.

Regardless of whether you are male or female, if you find that taking charge, planning and/or executing goals comes naturally to you, running masculine energy is easy for you.

By contrast, feminine or Yin energy is associated with intuitive, sensitive feeling. It is receptive, inwardly focused and delicate. You engage your feminine energy – yes, you men, too, and it does not make you "girly" – when you meditate, contemplate, reflect or simply allow yourself to be in silence and inaction.

Regardless of your sex, if you find it easy and natural to go with the flow without an agenda, to be receptive to your gut feelings, inner vision, inner voice and/or an unexplainable sense of knowing, you are well in touch with your feminine energy.

Your ability to run one type of energy may be more developed than the other, depending on your nature, your upbringing, your training, what you do for a living and your life experiences – overall, where you have more practice and what you feel more comfortable doing. Your sex does not automatically determine whether you are better versed at running your masculine or feminine energy.

For me, my educational and professional path had given me a lot more training and practice in accessing my masculine side. As a result, even though I have always been a girly-girl in appearance, especially in non-professional settings, I was more in my comfort zone when engaging my take-charge, directive, logical and get-things-done masculine energy. Even though, by nature, I am sensitive (an intuitive feeler, if you know temperament theory), I was a lot more comfortable showing my intellect than my deep capacities to feel. I had learned to trust logic and reasoning far more than my intuition and my ability to be still and know. In short, I was the poster child of a girly-girl rocking my Yang groove!

Alice P. Chan, Ph.D.

If you are a Star Wars fan, you know that there are dark and light sides to "the Force." (For the sake of full disclosure, I have never watched all the movies, but have always loved this metaphor!) The same goes for Yin and Yang energies.

With the light or healthy side of feminine energy, we tap into our empowering intuitive abilities, and allow the highest and wisest part of ourselves to come forward to tell us what we need to know. We are receptive to being still and waiting for inner guidance and inspiration. Meanwhile, feelings of insecurities, self-doubt and jealousy reside in the dark or unhealthy side of Yin energy.

With masculine energy, on the light, healthy side, we get results from meticulous planning, taking action and following through to goal completion. Again, think of the great breakthroughs in human history. Without masculine energy, the visions of the dreamers would not have come to fruition. When this Yang energy is used in an unhealthy way – the dark side – we see the much less desirable, and sometimes destructive, need to control people and our environment to keep ourselves safe.

Our risk-adverse ego thrives on the dark side of both Yin and Yang energies. This is one reason why unconsciously following the direction of our ego is never in our best interest.

Putting it altogether, too much of either type of energy is sub-optimal for manifesting your dreams. With too much masculine energy, you run the risk of steam-rolling through the REACH process without truly listening to the deeper calling within you. Acting for the sake of not standing still or to run away from the status quo comes from predominantly masculine energy running the show.

Meanwhile, too much feminine energy would mean lots of envisioning at best with little to no action. Furthermore, because our fears feed on the dark side of feminine energy, they keep us playing safe but unfortunately small. Being caught in a perpetual loop of having great vision, great ideas but little to no follow-through are telltale signs of feminine energy dominating the show.

In sum, a balanced approach – leveraging both the light side of Yin and Yang energies – is optimal for realizing our dreams. REACH engages *both* our receptivity to visioning and inner guidance through meditations and contemplation (feminine energy) *and* our active participation in manifesting our dreams by planning and taking strategic action (masculine energy).

Welcome Inner Voice, Ego in Check

Related to the above REACH principle, by engaging our feminine energy in a healthy, conscious manner, we practice being in a mode of receptivity, allowing the wisest and most creative part of ourselves to come forward and guide us.

We all have an inner voice that knows what is best for our highest good and what would fulfill our dreams. This inner voice is our biggest fan, champion, supporter and coach, and wants nothing more than for us to be blissfully happy and living joyously every day. When we take purposeful action following such inner guidance, we can walk boldly and confidently in the direction of our dreams.

Some of us may not be aware of this inner voice or may not trust it. Others seldom hear it, because we either have not been trained to pay attention to it or it is simply drowned out by the static and noise in our lives. We are often too pre-occupied with the fear-based actions prescribed by our inner critic – a.k.a. ego – whose primary interest is to ensure we survive.

Our inner critic is quick to call out anything we do that does not conform to the subconscious programming ingrained in our psyche, which can be full of limiting messages, fears and worries. Our ego does not like us taking risks and, therefore, stands ready to caution us for being too old, too young, too inexperienced, too ambitious, etc., to contemplate doing anything remotely outside of our comfort zone. Our ego's mission is to act as the director of our lives, lest we pay more attention to our inner voice guiding us to expand and grow, instead of remaining in the safety of the status quo.

With REACH, you will practice trusting the wise and loving inner voice within you that champions your expansion and your happiness. As you strengthen your clear connection to your inner wisdom, you will put your inner critic on notice. Provided you are ready and willing, the sabotaging old beliefs playing in your subconscious will be replaced by new empowering programming.

In the case of my book project, the message from my cautious ego for years was: *I am not qualified to write this book; No one would want to read it; I don't want to be humiliated.* Listening to that inner critic, I got discouraged from writing several times. When I got more practice in engaging the light side of my feminine energy, I became more tuned into the wise and encouraging inner voice of my soul. Eventually, what I heard instead was: *Finish REACH book. Just do it. You have a message to share. Don't delay.* Following this guidance from my inner voice, I engaged the healthy side of my masculine energy to finish the book you now hold in your hands.

You Cannot Fail with REACH

REACH honors the fact that you are exactly where you need to be at any given point in time. This process is designed to work for you, no matter where you are on your life path and what you are ready to do.

There is no referee, no timekeeper. You are completely in charge of your own destiny. Go at your own pace. As a rule of thumb, spend at least a week on each chapter, so that you can really work with the tools and let their results sink in. Spending one day per exercise is a good way to pace yourself. It does not matter whether you read the entire chapter first and then go back to do the exercises, or whether you complete them as you go along. As long as you fully engage in the exercises, you will reap the benefits of working with these tools.

Depending on what your dreams are relative to your present circumstances, you may find that you need more or less time with each chapter. Trust your inner compass. You will know if you are ready to move on to the next chapter or if you may want to revisit a particular exercise another day.

If you find that you need more time to work on releasing the limiting beliefs, fears and worries holding you back, by all means, do that. In fact, from my own experience and hearing that of many others, releasing often happens in layers over time. The longer you have lived, the more likely you will have layers of outdated beliefs to release. So, be patient with yourself, and honor what needs to happen in its time.

You cannot rush yourself when you are not ready to move onto the next step. If you push yourself too fast without a clear idea of what you want, you run a much higher risk of not seeing results and giving up altogether.

The important thing is to commit to staying with the roadmap – and coming back to it if you get sidetracked or discouraged. In the meantime, also pay attention to the improvements you will have made for yourself – and celebrate your progress. This sends a clear message to your subconscious that you mean business!

The quality of the results and where this process will take you depend solely on how much you are willing to own this personal discovery and transformation. I will not sugarcoat it and say that it will be smooth-sailing all the way. In fact, there will likely be times when it might seem too uncomfortable to continue. Such is the nature of change.

But, I promise you, if you stick with the whole process and really work it, the results will be well worth any discomfort. You will become more and more conscious of how you lead your life and learn how to *choose* your reality as you perceive it. Put another way, try to picture what it would be like if you ignore your inner call to go after a different life. Do you really want more of your current life or the one with your dreams fulfilled? REACH-ing your dreams is why you have picked up this book, isn't it?

How to Use this Book

To get the most out of this book, it is imperative that you do the exercises. Reading the principles and insights alone will not do much for you. You have to practice them in order to experience their power to change your life for the better.

I highly recommend that you get a notebook or a journal for your contemplations in this book. **You can also download a free copy of a companion workbook at dralicechan.com.** Of course, if you prefer to record them on your computer, please feel free to do so. What is critical is that you work with the tools in this book.

REACH is intended to shift your consciousness by replacing old, limiting beliefs with updated, empowering ones, and to help you take guided, inspired action to manifest your dreams. Therefore, please don't short-change yourself by skipping the true power and value of using this book. Instead, do yourself a favor, and set aside some quiet time to complete the exercises. Aren't your dreams worth this bit of dedication?

If you find yourself shying away from any of the exercises, notice that. When you are able to have a few moments of quiet time for reflection, ask yourself very gently why you are resisting it. What fear or discomfort is trying to get your attention?

Know that when we become aware of any fear or doubt, it is actually very good news – this fear is ready to be released. So, please don't be afraid of this happening, even though it does not feel good. This experience of coming face to face with resistance in and of itself could tell you something truly valuable about any blocks ready to be cleared on your path to your dreams.

In sum, please don't judge yourself for feeling any resistance as you embark on your REACH journey. It is very natural for old limiting messages to surface when going through change. Acknowledge yourself for having the clarity and the insight to recognize a fear or worry you are ready to release in order to get one step closer to your dreams.

Setting Your Conscious Intention

As we get ready to begin our REACH journey together, let me ask you to take a moment to contemplate and journal on the following two questions:

- What do you hope to get out of this book?
- What dream do you hope to realize? (If you have more than one, pick the one you want the most at this point.)

Based on what you will have written, you are going to set an intention. By intention, I mean a conscious purpose you would like to fulfill by using this book. For example, if your dream is to have a more satisfying career, and you hope that working with this book will help you get closer to fulfilling this dream, then this is your intention. In your journal or workbook, complete the following *Intention Statement*:

- My intention for working with this book is to:

    _____

    _____

Look at your intention statement every time you pick up this book to continue where you left off. This keeps your intention front and center in your consciousness.

As a final recommendation to wrap up this introduction to REACH, please honor yourself and where you are always. You will read more about *Honor* in Chapter 6. But let me make the key point about *Honor* here as it relates to working with REACH: Please don't let what you do or don't do with REACH be a source of guilt or bad feelings about yourself.

If you get side-tracked and take a long break from working with this book, honor the distractions and your need to take care of life. Just come back when you are ready to resume.

Remember the intention you just set about why you want to work with this book. You have a desire to change your life for the better in some way. Let's keep that intention in mind. Give yourself full and complete permission to imagine a better life, and go confidently in the direction of your dreams – all in a way that suits *you and where you are*!

Summary Points for Introduction to REACH

❖ Emotional and physical safety is the most basic human need. Dreaming is a higher-order desire that cannot easily flourish unless the foundation of safety is established. That is why when our life is full of fear and doubt, it is challenging to get clear about what we want, let alone imagine a better life with dreams fulfilled.

❖ Our path to realizing our dreams is often filled with roadblocks. These blocks are limiting beliefs, fears and worries we have inadvertently accumulated since we were young children. Until we become aware of these blocks and release them, they generate repetitive life patterns.

❖ A key ingredient to manifesting our dreams is taking action. Dreaming and thinking positively alone are not sufficient. Taking guided action that is aligned with a clear intention is a critical part of the formula for manifesting our dreams.

❖ REACH is a personal empowerment roadmap consisting of five parts: *Release, Envision, Act, Celebrate* and *Honor*.

❖ REACH steps you through how to be a match for your dreams, i.e., the woman/man for whom you want to be loved, the colleague for whom you want to be valued, the best caregiver to your heart, mind, body and soul you could manifest.

❖ REACH is a non-linear process that honors life as a labyrinth. You can stay as long as you want in each of the five components or jump around as necessary. Just like the windy path of a labyrinth eventually takes you to the center goal, if you trust REACH and work with the steps, it will take you to your dreams.

- ❖ REACH uses a balanced approach, by engaging *both* our receptivity to visioning and inner guidance through meditations and contemplation (feminine energy) *and* our active participation in manifesting our dreams by planning and taking strategic action (masculine energy).

- ❖ By practicing REACH, we learn to trust our inner voice, which comes from the highest and most creative part of ourselves. We learn to choose to listen to it over the self-sabotaging urges coming from our inner critic – a.k.a. ego – whose job is to keep us safe but playing small.

- ❖ You simply cannot fail with REACH, because you personally own this process. No one is there to judge you, and what you get is a result of what you are ready to put in. Pace yourself. Take at least one week per chapter, or as long as it feels right to you.

- ❖ Honor yourself through this process. Don't rush yourself through it or push yourself too hard, lest you get discouraged and give up altogether. Don't let REACH become another reason to feel guilty, or like a failure for not doing something in this process for any reason.

- ❖ Read your Intention Statement every time you come back to this book to do more.

CHAPTER 2

Release

*"The longer we dwell on our misfortunes,
the greater is their power to harm us."*
— *Voltaire*

For a good part of 2009, I struggled with the physical and psychological recovery from the accident you read about in the *Prologue*. Dizziness was my daily companion, and I limped along with a fraction of my normal strength. Some days, aside from feeling physically ill, I felt extremely lonely and afraid. I nearly wished I had just died in the accident, as *that* would have been easier. It took every ounce of energy I could muster up to barely get through each day – just to do it all over again the next day.

By late spring, I was fed up with living like that, done with feeling that it took all I had merely to survive. I was determined to thrive again. I remembered the Presence that held me with love in the hospital, and that there was a greater life purpose awaiting my fulfillment. I dug deep into my inner reserve, and my energy gradually started shifting. I began to get stronger physically, too.

Shortly after I set my intention to thrive again, I found great inspiration from David Cook's "*Time of My Life.*" It seemed like this song would come on the radio magically, whenever I could use a shot of inspiration. It perfectly echoed how I felt and cheered me on, that it was time for me to step into what I was kept alive to do. The opening verse particularly got me pumped up:

> "I've been waiting for my dreams to turn into
> Something I could believe in.
> Looking for that magic rainbow on the horizon,
> I couldn't see it.
> Until I let go, gave into love,
> And watched all my bitterness burn.
> Now, I'm coming alive body and soul,
> Feeling my world start to turn."

In order for my reality to change for the better, I first needed to release the negativity in my energy field: (1) fearful feelings of having lost control of my life – literally in the accident and metaphorically in being held hostage by the recovery process; (2) years of cumulative resentment and bitterness about my stagnating career; and (3) any and all excuses for why I could not pursue the life of my dreams.

I needed to release all disempowering thoughts, feelings and beliefs keeping me from stepping into my soul's calling. I needed to dissolve the stranglehold my fears and worries had over my destiny.

In the *Introduction* chapter, we discussed briefly how fears keep us in survival mode. They use up all of our mental capacity and emotional resources, leaving little to no fuel for our dream engine. We learned that fears often stem from limiting beliefs that are deeply ingrained in our subconscious, unknowingly blocking our path to realizing our dreams.

In this chapter, we will dive deeper into identifying and releasing the roadblocks on our path. We will look at how fears, worries and limiting beliefs build inadvertently, and how to recognize the telltale signs that we are ready to release the negativity blocking our creative flow.

We will work with tools to reveal and clear out these blocks, making room to foster empowering beliefs that are aligned with our dreams.

Whose Line Is It Anyway?

Have you ever watched this live TV program that aired from 1998 to 2006? It was a very entertaining show of improvisational comedy. The actors on the show were given the premise of a series of scenes, along with the basic description of each character in each scene. Their job was to play out real-time the roles assigned to them, following the story premise. There was no script, nor did they have time to think about how to act out their parts or to rehearse. The overall quality of the skits depended on the actors' spontaneous creative interpretation of their roles within the boundaries of the plot, and how well each actor improvised in response to what his/her counterparts did.

I find this show to be a great metaphor for life, except in a less slapstick sort of way. Let's deconstruct this, shall we?

We were all born into some sort of a storyline already set up, along with the roles to which we were assigned and people with whom we were meant to play out the story. The premise of the skit represents the trajectory of our lives, launching off of the beginning circumstances into which we were born.

For instance, you may have been born into a suburban middle-class family, growing up comfortably in a safe environment. You were raised with expectations – spoken or unspoken – to continue the tradition, i.e., creating a middle-class life of your own with family, community, stability and financial security.

Or, you may have been born into poverty in an inner city, or amidst socio-economic and political turmoil. You learned since a young age that life was uncertain and maybe even dangerous, that you needed to fend for yourself and fight for everything you wanted.

These are just a couple of examples of what a story premise may entail; the variations are endless. The point is that we were all set up in one way or another according to the circumstances into which we were born.

From there, how we each play out our story depends on our interpretation of our assigned role and our ability to improvise – using the skills we consciously cultivate through formal education and life experiences. More importantly, though, just as the quality of the acting on *"Whose Line Is It Anyway?"* hinged on how much the actors inherently *believed* they were creative and talented, our ability to improvise in the story of our lives also depends on our own self-beliefs. And, just like the comedians bounced off each others' acting to complete a specific skit, our life is also shaped by how our actions interplay real-time with those of our counterparts – no scripts, no rehearsals.

Each of our roles also comes with character guidelines. These guidelines represent the messages we carry with us about ourselves and the world in which we live. These messages are reinforced through interactions with other people with their own roles to play. Our acting counterparts are first our parents, siblings, friends, teachers and other authority figures, and, later in life, significant others, in-laws, bosses, colleagues and business partners.

Some of these messages are positive and encouraging, inspiring us to believe and dream, that the world is a friendly place, full of possibilities, wonder and magic. Other messages lead us to believe subconsciously that we are less powerful, creative and capable than we truly are, that the world is less trustworthy, supportive and cooperative than it really is.

Do you know that negative messages and experiences are five times as likely as positive ones to register and stay with us? It takes truly amazing positive experiences to be equally powerful. That is why leading relationship expert, Dr. John Gottman, author of *The Seven*

Principles for Making Marriage Work, recommends the five-to-one rule to couples: For every negative thought or belief we have about our partner, we need to identify five positive things we appreciate about them to offset that one negative belief.

We have this negativity bias because part of our brain – the amygdala – is wired for survival. Anything that potentially threatens our fundamental sense of safety and security is intrinsically more memorable. After all, our survival instincts want us to be ready to fight, run or freeze – whichever restores our feelings of safety.

As mentioned in Chapter 1, when we are busy achieving or restoring feelings of safety, we have no capacity for higher-level desires. This is why it is so critical for us to bring limiting beliefs – expressed through their associated fears and worries – to the forefront to be released.

For some messages that are deeply ingrained within us, it may take a little more processing before we are ready to let them go. We may have to first identify the source of these beliefs, when in our lives we inadvertently acquired them, and for what purpose they served that are now outdated.

By processing tenacious old beliefs this way, we honor the fact that they served a purpose in the past, but that we have long since outgrown them. In doing so, we unlock the grip these beliefs have on us, so that we can truly let them go. We will get to some techniques of how to process and release old beliefs later in this chapter.

Beliefs we internalized as young children are often the ones we tend to forget, but yet are still active in our subconscious mind, shaping what we believe about the life we deserve to live.

Claire Zammit, a cofounder of *Feminine Power* (www.femininepower.com), said that when we were kids, we lacked the sophistication to make sense of events and circumstances. As a result, we might misinterpret experiences we were having at home or at school as indications of our self-worth. We might come to view trouble at home as a sign of us being bad, or to expect everyone we meet in our adult lives to be as doting as our parents.

Whatever the specifics may be, until we are conscious of the childhood messages about ourselves we accumulated, we continue to unknowingly let them shape what we believe as adults. And, as we discussed in Chapter 1, we cannot address subconscious old beliefs by overlaying positive thoughts on top of them. We need to become aware of them and release their control over how we live.

A Case of Familial and Cultural Messages

To illustrate the above discussion about old beliefs from early in life, let me tell you a personal story. My parents were born in Asia around World War II, and they both had truly heartbreaking, depriving childhoods. My dad had a junior high education, while my mom barely finished elementary school. But, to this day, they are two of the most curious people I have ever known in my life, and they truly love to learn.

My mom reads voraciously, and keeps up with current events as if her life depends on it. She used to be mistaken for a school teacher all the time, because she had that air about her. My early childhood memories of my dad included him studying all the time. He was always working toward some professional certification in order to make up for his lack of formal education. He also had a great interest in learning foreign languages.

I am truly fortunate to have come from such strong lines of curious and diligent genes, which really set me up nicely for success in life. I will forever be grateful for all the formal education I am so lucky to have; my parents were not so fortunate.

I believe my parents truly did the best they could possibly do, given their upbringing and life circumstances. Objectively speaking, however, there was a lot of talk about lack in my household when I was growing up. The energy of struggle and fear permeated my childhood home.

In hindsight, I am in awe of how well my mom was able to stretch money and resources. She was always talking about what we could not afford and how we needed to conserve. For constantly feeling there was not enough, she did an amazing job in getting the family fed and clothed, and all four of us kids educated at good schools, so that we could grow up to have better lives. I honestly doubt if I could have done as well as my mom did if I were in her shoes.

On top of family circumstances, I grew up in a culture with a rich history of glorifying suffering and perseverance. Sacrificing the present for the future was a great virtue, especially when it came to saving money. I remember vividly a bank commercial I watched all the time as a kid that urged people to save, that storing water one drop at a time ultimately creates a river.

As a child, I was extremely sensitive. I hated being a disappointment to anyone, especially authority figures. Consequently, since a very young age, I internalized the collective messages from my family and my cultural background. What got programmed into my subconscious was a deeply ingrained fear that I could never save enough to make up for the lack in life. Furthermore, spending money was grossly irresponsible and would make me a bad person.

As I became more established in my adult life, I continued to be frugal and conservative with money. It had become second nature for me to ask: *Can I afford this now? Do I really need this now?* I rarely asked myself what I wanted, as wanting was a frivolous luxury.

But, as time went by, I began to question if it was actually wrong to want. Furthermore, I started wondering: *When does the present actually stop and the future begin? When can I finally stop sacrificing and start enjoying life?* As I learned more and more about the importance of releasing resistance – another term for roadblocks – and allowing abundance to flow in my life, my subconscious beliefs about lack needed to go as well.

When I took the time to assess where my beliefs about money came from (my childhood) and what purpose they served (trying to create a sense of security and honoring authority figures), I was able to dissolve the stranglehold of my irrational fears. What I have retained instead are the healthy practices of responsible money management, which include following a spending plan that allows me to enjoy living in the present, while continuing to save for the long term.

Releasing Outdated Messages

So, it actually serves a dual purpose to start this section of the chapter with the question, "*Whose line is it anyway?*" First, as you read above, it provides a metaphor for framing where some of our oldest and often hidden beliefs actually originate – the story premise into which we were born, the roles we were assigned to play and the characters with whom to act out the story spontaneously.

The second purpose is for us to ask literally – *Whose line is it anyway?* – whenever a message surfaces guiding us on how to act and how to make decisions. In my example above, the lines were: *I can't afford this; It's irresponsible for me to spend this money.*

You may have similar messages or others. Whatever your specific message(s) are, ask yourself these questions:

- Whose line is it anyway? Is it mine at present time? Or is it a line from forgotten childhood experiences – perhaps from adults or authority figures – I had inadvertently internalized and believed as my truth?

- Who am I trying to honor by living by this line?

- How does it serve me now to repeat this line and to let it guide me in how I live my life?

Please allow me to clarify a critical point here. By asking you to consider the source of the limiting messages trapped in your subconscious, I do not advocate that you blame anyone, whether your parents or somebody else. Blaming will not help you release old beliefs, but can unnecessarily damage relationships. It is precisely the opposite of what I want for you. After all, consider that others have their own latent limiting beliefs driving *their* behavior – and they do not know that.

So, I urge you to be willing to take responsibility for your own destiny, by dispelling the myth of any guiding principle that is not your truth and that which does not serve you anymore – all without needing to make someone else wrong.

You are in a very powerful position to be able to *choose* only those messages and beliefs that align with what you want to be in your life. I urge you to exercise this powerful personal choice!

O *Contemplation Exercise*

- Think about your dream. What is the first message of "*I can't do this because...*" that comes to mind? Write that in your journal or workbook.

- Now, proceed to answer the above three questions, starting with "Whose line is it anyway?"

Recognizing What to Release

We just looked at how we may have forgotten limiting beliefs. If we are unaware of them, how can we let them go? Let's talk about how to recognize when something is ready to be released. We will be working with a number of contemplation exercises to uncover some old beliefs. Please pace yourself on these exercises, and do not rush through them. Give yourself the time to do them and the space to break between them.

Remember, if you resist any of these exercises, notice it without judging yourself. It is perfectly ok. When you are ready, ask yourself what feelings were triggered and/or what you were trying to avoid. We will talk more about triggers and avoidance below.

Where Is Your Focus?

To begin this section, we are going to do a simple exercise. Please have your journal or workbook ready.

O *Contemplation Exercise*

Think of the most recent substantive interaction you had with someone in your life that lasted longer than a few minutes. This person is more than just an acquaintance, but instead your partner, a friend, colleague or family member. This interaction could be in person, on the phone, or over email.

Contemplate the following questions, and journal on your answers:

- What did you talk about? What was/were the dominant theme(s) in your interaction?
  - Did you bask in all the things that were going well in your lives? Did you share exciting possibilities on the horizon, such as job leads, a new love interest, etc.?
  - Did you take turns recounting in microscopic detail the latest stressful work situation, relationship woe or family drama – or all of the above?
- How does it feel to remember that interaction? Does it remind you of how energized you were coming away from

that wonderful sharing, or are you all tensed up again, reliving the draining venting session?

- How does this interaction compare to other encounters in your life? Is this interaction typical, or is it an unusual occurrence?

- What did you get from this simple recall exercise? What does it say about your dominant focus?

Where we focus our time and energy says a lot about what we project out and, in turn, draw back into our lives. Events and people reflect back to us what is active in the magnetic field of our beliefs, perspective and outlook.

If we are grounded in our lives, grateful for what we have, excited for the possibilities around the corner, we naturally find ourselves surrounded by people with similar perspectives and outlooks.

When struggles and drama are dominant in our lives, we find ourselves among those with whom to commiserate. After all, misery loves company, right? Actually, it is simply that like attracts like. Quite simply, have you noticed that it is easier to be with others who share your beliefs and outlooks than those who have vastly different perspectives than yours?

Some of us may think that, by stewing in the negativity in each other's lives, we offer each other support and relief. We may even justify repeatedly telling our loved ones grievance stories as keeping them informed of our lives. But who really needs to know in great detail the latest drama in your cousin's life whom they have barely met? Who is really missing out on your life if they do not hear blow by blow how every person at your job gets mistreated by your mean boss – when all these people are strangers to the listener? The "who" are those apt to reciprocate with similar stories of their own.

The point of this exercise is to have you pay attention to where you place your focus. This consciousness-building practice is *not* aimed at calling out other people being negative. Rather, it is about becoming more aware of what energy *you* project out that attracts people and events to mirror back to you the beliefs, perspective and outlook *you* offer.

If people and experiences in your life are mostly negative, your radio receiver is tuned into a station of negative programming. It is up to you to change the dial by changing the frequencies of your own thoughts and feelings.

In *The Four Spiritual Laws of Prosperity: A Simple Guide to Unlimited Abundance*, Edwene Gaines issues a 21-day challenge to rid ourselves of negativity. If you accept the challenge, for 21 straight days, there will be no complaining, criticizing, gossiping or negative speech of any kind.

Even if you feel the urge to complain, criticize or talk about the outrageous thing someone did, as long as you do not verbalize it, you are meeting the challenge. However, as soon as you slip and say something negative, the calendar resets – even on Day 20 – and the 21 day count starts all over again. What is the magic to 21 days? It is how long it takes to habituate a new practice.

Whether or not you decide to take on this precise 21-day challenge, it is a good idea to pay attention to what you talk about day in and day out. When you start taking notice of your everyday thought patterns as reflected in your conversations with others, you become aware of whether negativity runs on automatic pilot in your daily life.

What Pushes Your Buttons?

The precise things that irritate, frustrate or make us uncomfortable are triggers for old beliefs or unhealed wounds that surface in our consciousness to be addressed and released. If we don't realize this, we will continue to be triggered, until we deal with the source of the trigger. Therefore, one way to identify what beliefs need to go is to notice what pushes our buttons.

For example, it used to irritate me a great deal when people were unresponsive to my emails. I felt ignored and disrespected. Consideration of common courtesy aside, unbeknownst to me, this behavior triggered a forgotten childhood wound: *People ignored me, because I did not count as a girl. My needs did not matter. I did not matter.*

When I became aware of this button, I was able to take others' non-response less personally. They had *their* reasons, whatever those might be, which had nothing to do with me.

In his book, *A New Earth*, Eckhart Tolle says that we have a pain-body. This pain-body accumulates unhealed wounds from experiences over the course of our lives. These wounds could be hurtful childhood experiences that affected our self-esteem, adult relationship pain, career upsets and other disappointments in life.

For many of us, this pain-body operates beneath the radar of our consciousness. Consequently, we unknowingly attract people whose own pain triggers a familiar response within us, activating similar pain we ourselves experienced.

Until we are cognizant of our pain-body, we continue the cycle of attracting others' pain to feed our own pain-body. Think about repeating the same heartbreaking relationship patterns or the same stressful, unfulfilling jobs. By becoming aware of our forgotten wounds, by healing them and releasing the pain, we stop repeating the life patterns necessary to feed our pain-body.

It is a misnomer that others *make* us feel bad. Others' actions might set off certain emotional response within us, if we are not aware of our buttons and allow ourselves to be triggered. However, it is always our choice as to whether and how to react.

Alice P. Chan, Ph.D.

Wouldn't you want to understand why certain behavior really pushes your buttons? At a deeper level, wouldn't you want to dissolve the magnetic charge in your subconscious that attracts the same painful relationship, stressful job, or unpleasant life circumstance over and over again? Wouldn't you want to tune your radio receiver to more positive, empowering frequencies?

Whether we are irritated by people always being late, are devastated time and again by infidelity on the part of different partners, or feel like a perpetual spineless doormat in our professional life, our emotional reactions are very good indicators for what we harbor that need to be released.

To give you an example, for years, I kept attracting men into my life who were intimidated by my education and academic achievements, especially being a former award-winning Cornell professor. Then, one day, while venting to a friend about yet another guy in my life expressing his discomfort with the academic gap between us, my friend asked, "Are *you* comfortable with how educated you are and what you have achieved?"

At first, that seemed like the most ridiculous question she could have asked me. My reflex was to say, "Of course, I am!" But, when I honestly reflected on my friend's question later, I was shocked to realize that I was not completely comfortable with my own academic achievements and what I had accomplished.

You see, I grew up in a culture at a time when boys were a lot more valued than girls. The message I repeatedly received since a very young age was that I was inferior to my three brothers because I was a girl, that I would never do as well as they would do, that I did not *deserve* as much as they did. Even up until I was in college, I was told I was not as smart as the boys in my family, that I would need a college education to compete with a high school graduate for a job.

With year after year of having these messages drilled into my head – and my heart – I had come to believe in my innate inferiority and inherent lack of worth. I was destined to have to work harder than others to earn the same right to a decent life. As a result, for much of my life, I blindly did everything I could to compensate for my lack of self-worth, working really hard to earn my place in this life.

In the process, I accomplished a lot, because I felt I had a lot to prove. However, I also ended up tiptoeing around my academic achievements, not fully owning my personal power and intelligence, because they contradicted my longstanding subconscious beliefs of inferiority and unworthiness.

Until I became aware of these buried wounds and hidden beliefs I had internalized about myself, I kept repeating the same pattern of attracting men who were uncomfortable with my intelligence and accomplishments – and ultimately with me.

The men I subconsciously called into my life were mirrors reflecting back to me my own dissonance and inability to really see, accept and love myself. These men showed up in my life to feed the pain-body within me and to catalyze my learning of my own truth. That is, I deserve love and acceptance as much as anybody else – and not because I had earned these privileges, but because I am deserving, period.

However, first, I must believe in myself, celebrate the woman I have become, before the external circumstances of my life will line up to reflect back to me how I see myself. When I released those old beliefs of inadequacies, stepped into the gifts with which I was born to serve, and embraced my hard-earned achievements with humble pride, I stopped attracting men who were intimidated by me and what I have accomplished.

Alice P. Chan, Ph.D.

○ *Contemplation Exercise*

- In what ways do others push your buttons? Why does their behavior irritate you?

- What negative patterns, if any, repeat in your life – personal, professional, health, financial, etc.? What underlying beliefs do you think generate these life patterns?

The above exercise is intended to help you start building awareness for your hidden old beliefs and your pain-body. Once you are aware of them, you can take steps to dissolve their charge. Again, we will be talking about release tools later in this chapter.

What Are You Trying To Avoid?

Just like our buttons and repetitive life patterns show us beliefs we need to release, what we try to avoid also tells us about fears that block our path to growth and a bigger life. In *The Big Leap*, Dr. Gay Hendricks says that all of us have a "Zone of Genius," though most of us may not be aware of it and do not live there. In this zone, we fulfill our life purpose by being the best and most creative version of ourselves, doing what truly lights us up, not just where we have demonstrated competence or even excellence.

Moving into this Zone of Genius requires us to stretch ourselves, so it is uncomfortable, and it will likely trigger fear. When we are afraid to step outside of our comfort zone and repeatedly resist it, our subconscious mind – our radio tuner – may call in an excuse for us to stay right where we are in the form of an illness or an accident. When we are down from being sick or injured, we have the perfect, albeit unpleasant, excuse to avoid doing what scares us.

In October 2003, a huge SUV ploughed into my car from behind, pushing it into the car in front of mine. That car went under the car in front, before a fifth car was hit. It was four days before my first wedding anniversary. My marriage was failing, and I was haunted by the same nightmare night after night about this reality that I did not want to accept. My ex-husband is a very thoughtful, generous and congenial man, but we were just not right for each other. We attempted to stay together and had been in counseling for months trying to save our marriage.

However, deep down I knew that, just as we got married for the wrong reasons, we would be staying together for the wrong reasons, too. We were supposed to go away for the weekend to celebrate our anniversary. But I dreaded doing that, as it just felt hypocritical to me. Being bed-ridden for back injuries, I had the perfect excuse for not celebrating what was on its way out of my life – even if it would take another few months before I had the stomach to accept it.

Similarly, the accident in December 2008 was another case of major avoidance. It was after my Sedona visit in March of the same year, and I had been introduced to my Zone of Genius – doing REACH work. I knew I needed to leave the job I had long since outgrown, but was too frozen in place by worries about how I would sustain my life. As much as I was miserable professionally, it was easier to ignore what I needed to do and to continue tolerating the familiar pain.

And guess what? That horrendous accident required me to focus on getting myself back to health and strength. It was the perfect excuse not to leave my comfort zone and step into my Zone of Genius.

During the time of both accidents, there were significant life changes I needed to make. However, I was too paralyzed by fear to take action. So, the universe delivered the accidents as answers to the fear-based requests from my subconscious – to have the perfect excuses to avoid what I lacked the courage to do.

Those were very costly and painful excuses, of course, but they bought me time to avoid what frightened me to my core. In both cases, the accidents also ended up being blaring wakeup calls that really got my attention. It was time to let go of the fears that kept me settling for controlled misery.

Having learned my lesson, when I felt the inner nudge repeatedly to leave my job in November 2009 to become self-employed, I did not resist it. My logical mind – and my fearful ego – warned me that the year-end was a lousy time to try to generate business for a new consulting practice. However, I knew better than to question the November timeframe that repeatedly came to me.

So, I left my job just before Thanksgiving. And, even though I did not know at the time how things would work out, I ended up having my highest income-earning year in 2010, working a lot less and feeling much more appreciated than in my entire career working for someone else. I leapt, and faith rewarded me with a great net to catch me. I said "Yes" to my soul's calling to leave that which no longer served me, and the frequencies of my faith called in greater abundance and ease to match my evolved internal state.

Ultimately, I am truly grateful for the personal breakthroughs brought by these two accidents, and I genuinely honor their places on my life path that brought me to this point. However, would I *consciously* court such rude awakenings? Not in a million years!

I've learned that we do not get to choose what lessons we come into this life to learn. However, we have a choice in *how* we learn them, either through great pain or great love.

So, take it from someone who learned it the hard way, if you want to avoid anything, avoid attracting traumatic excuses by answering your call to change, even if just taking one baby step at a time. You do not need to undertake a drastic overhaul immediately, unless you want to do that, of course. However, it would be wise to start taking steps toward the change you are called to make.

When your soul knows that you are ready to grow, your inner wisdom will continue to nudge you to stretch yourself, to break through old limiting beliefs and life patterns. Know that when you repeatedly resist the call to grow, you are defaulting to the choice of growing through pain. Take baby steps toward what is calling you or face a harsher awakening. My stories demonstrated that. Maybe you or someone you know have similar stories.

So, please do yourself a favor. When you feel a gnawing sense that something in your life needs to change, listen to it. It is your inner wisdom nudging you to make a change for the better. What you need to do may scare you, but know that it is ultimately for your highest good. The wisest and most creative part of you knows that you are ready for it. And you are never given more than you can handle.

If you repeatedly ignore this call to grow, it will get louder and louder. Eventually, your subconscious may do you a very clumsy favor, by calling in an avoidance excuse that is much more uncomfortable than the change you try to avoid – before you end up having to change anyway.

Just keep in sight your grand prize for saying "Yes" to your call: Being deliriously happy living the life of your dreams!

○ *Contemplation Exercise*

- What changes, if any, are you trying to avoid? What fears are behind this avoidance?

Intermission

I know we are not at the opera or a live performance, but let's have an intermission anyway. How are you doing? We have done some deep dives into likely some really uncomfortable territory, and you should be mighty proud of yourself! I know this firsthand, and I want to congratulate you on the great work you have done. The first steps to releasing what does not serve you are awareness and willingness. And, you have shown up with both in flying colors. Bravo!

For our intermission, I want to offer you an inspirational message. Do you know that butterflies symbolize new beginnings? Do you also know that when a butterfly first emerges from its cocoon, it struggles, strains and presses against the walls of its cocoon? The struggling and straining pump fluid from the over-sized body of the young butterfly into its newly formed wings that are weak. This process simultaneously strengthens the wings and reduces the size of the unwieldy body. Without the initial struggles, the butterfly cannot fly, nor can it survive.

What a great metaphor for life: The struggles we experience ultimately enable us to break free from the confines of our cocoon and fly to a life of beauty and prosperity.

Revealing, Updating and Replacing Old Agreements

Welcome back from our intermission. We are going to start the second half of this chapter by engaging solely our receptive feminine energy to access our subconscious.

Below is a guided meditation that will reveal some old, forgotten agreements you made with yourself at some point in your life that matched your situation then. They served a purpose at the time, but no longer serve you now or where you want to go in life. You may have forgotten about them, but they are still active in the magnetic field of your subconscious mind.

Read the steps in the meditation a few times over, so that you can guide yourself through it. You may also consider recording it, so that you can meditate to the recording.

○ *Meditation Exercise*

Treasure Chest Meditation[4]

- Close your eyes, and take several slow, deep breaths. With each breath in, imagine your body being gradually filled up with the most powerful, cleansing energy. With each breath out, feel your body releasing any tension, stress or discomfort. Repeat this breathing until you feel relaxed and grounded, and your mind is quiet.

- See yourself going to a favorite place of yours. You love this place, and you feel perfectly safe here.

- Once you have settled yourself comfortably, see a treasure chest in front of you. Take a moment to notice what it looks like – size, color, material, construction, etc.

- Ask the treasure chest to be filled with old agreements or promises you made with yourself at some point that don't serve you anymore.

- Open the treasure chest, slowly pull out an item, and ask the following questions:
    – What agreement or promise does this item represent?
    – When was this agreement or promise made?
    – What purpose did it serve?

---
[4] Adapted from a meditation by Bella Shing.

- Take out the next item, and repeat the above three questions.

- Repeat the above questions with all remaining items in the treasure chest.

- When you are done with all the items, ask that the agreements which no longer serve you be released. Ask that the outdated agreements be updated to match where you want to be in your life.

- Take note of your new, updated agreements. What are they?

In your journal or workbook, create two columns. In the first column, write the heading, "Old agreements/promises." Under it, as best you can remember, list the insights you got from the meditation about old agreements. In the second column, write the heading, "Released or updated agreements," and note which of the agreements in the first column were released and which ones were updated.

Now that you have recorded what you remember from the meditation, take a few moments to reflect on the insights and feelings you got from any part of the meditation. How was it for you? What did you see that surprised you, if at all? If the meditation made you uncomfortable, why? Did the release and update of old agreements make you feel lighter? Journal on your reactions.

○ *Contemplation Exercise*

Next, we are going to do some "hot penning." Set a timer for 10 minutes, and write whatever comes to mind in response to the following question:

- What fears, worries or beliefs are holding you back from living your dream?

Without judgment or censoring, keep writing whatever comes to mind, taking note of any accompanying feelings. Don't stop writing. Make a list if that resonates with you more. Don't worry about grammar, incomplete sentences, spelling, etc., as no one will be reading this. Keep writing from a stream of consciousness until the timer goes off.

Looking at what was revealed to you through your hot penning session about barriers to your dream, answer <u>one</u> of the following questions. Pick the one that resonates with you the most:

- What would the Higher Power of your understanding (e.g., God, Spirit, Source, etc.) say to you about each of these barriers?

- Imagine that these barriers plague someone you absolutely love, adore and believe in wholeheartedly. What would you say to her/him about each barrier that is keeping her/him from being the great success that you KNOW s/he is?

- Be your own "Devil's Advocate." Find evidence for why each barrier to your dream is simply not true.

Again, don't judge or censor what comes up for you. When you are done, look at your answers, and journal on any reactions that might have come up in this exercise. Did you expect to see these barriers, or did some of them surprise you? Why? Did you feel resistance to any part of this exercise? If so, why? How did it feel to invalidate the roadblocks that scare you so much? How did it help you to feel more empowered?

Release Rituals

Now that you have revealed the fears and beliefs blocking your path, you are ready to dissolve their charge. Let's send a clear message to your subconscious that you are done with the fears or beliefs. Choose a release ritual that is meaningful to you. Here are some suggestions:

- Write a letter turning over these old beliefs and fears to the universe, God, or any Higher Power of your understanding.

  I like to literally release mine into the ether, as the Divine is omnipresent energy to me. So, I write an email for my release ritual. Years ago, I created an email address that I named Divine Love. Sometimes, when I feel scared, or have a question that I want to ask, I send an email to this address. When I really need some comfort, I would log into that email account, get quiet and be in a receptive mode, and let the Divine speak through the highest part of me, my inner voice.

  If this practice resonates with you, go ahead and create your own direct electronic connection to the higher power of your understanding.

- Go into meditation, starting with the grounding step we went through above in the Treasure Chest Meditation. Picture all the fears and beliefs you are ready to release being pumped into a big red balloon. Red is the color of the energy center in your body that is associated with safety and security when it is not blocked by negative energy. So, red is meaningful. However, feel free to choose any color that resonates with you.

  When you are done filling up this balloon with what you want to release, tie it up and let it rise into the sky. When the balloon has reached a high enough altitude, picture yourself pulling out an extra long needle and popping the balloon. Watch all your worries and fears disappear into thin air.

- List the fears and worries you want to release on a separate sheet of paper. Burn it (safely, please!), and watch all these barriers to your dreams disintegrate into ashes. If it is meaningful for you to spread the ashes somewhere symbolic, do so.

Again, the above are just some ideas. Choose something to ritualize the release of the barriers to your dream. Do something that activates for you the feelings of completion with that which no longer serves you, giving you a sense of "*I am done with this roadblock on my path for good!*"

If you found the preceding release exercises challenging to complete, below is an easy and powerful tool to uncover and release fears and limiting beliefs. Even if you have success with the above exercises, you will still find the practice I am about to share with you extremely valuable to add to your REACH-Your-Dreams tool kit. It has been a great addition for mine.

Tap Your Way Out of Negativity and Into Self-Empowerment

One of the most powerful release tools I have used with great success is the Emotional Freedom Technique (EFT).[5] It is a very simple yet potent healing technique that combines tapping on energy points in our body with positive psychology.

I am introducing EFT here because it is easy to learn and practice on your own, as I have experienced. This technique is also a really

---

5 There's a wealth of information online on EFT and Meridian Tapping, including www.thetappingsolution.com and www.eftuniverse.com.

fast and dramatic way to let go of the negative emotions blocking our energy flow. After all, according to Gary Craig, founder of EFT, all negative emotions are ultimately caused by a disruption of the energy flow in our body. Even physical ailments are ultimately tied to energetic blockages.

Nick Ortner of The Tapping Solution says that tapping is a great way to process deep emotions and old beliefs, starting with where we are and what we are ready to do – very consistent with my REACH philosophy. If we are not yet ready to let go of a tenacious belief completely, that is perfectly fine. We can just begin with being consciously *willing* to detach from that belief and to work on letting it go progressively. When we are willing, this technique can really speed up the release and healing process.

EFT involves tapping on a number of meridian points in our body's energy system, while accepting ourselves unconditionally. By applying gentle yet firm pressure to these points through tapping, it triggers the release of stress, anxiety, pain, discomfort and other negative energy trapped in our body. Together with verbally acknowledging the condition troubling us without judgment, allowing whatever feelings we have about it to surface, we gradually release these emotions and the associated limiting beliefs.

Again, our *willingness* to let them go is key. As we continue to tap and affirm our unconditional self-acceptance, we stimulate more release of the trapped negative energy, until it is completely cleared from our system. In turn, we allow passage for the flow of an improved condition. Our mind follows by looking for and registering supporting evidence of the improvement, thereby paving the way for new empowering beliefs.

In short, we can tap our way out of the roadblocks to our dreams and into creating new affirming beliefs aligned with where we want to go.

I stumbled upon EFT when I was in search of a cure for chronic eczema on my face I had endured for two years. (See Appendix to read more about my experience.) What I got ended up being much more than a cure to the physical condition. EFT ultimately helped me to shift my core beliefs, and complemented my spiritual practice in unblocking my energy channels to allow inner guidance to flow.

Components of the Treatment

I am not formally trained to practice EFT on others. So, in this section, I will walk you through the steps I took to treat myself. If this technique resonates with you, let me encourage you to learn more about it on your own and try it for yourself. There are lots of resources on the Web to show you how you can practice EFT on your own. I have listed some resources in this book to help you get started.

If you find it challenging to uncover hidden fears or to process and release tenacious old beliefs, working with an EFT practitioner in your local area can be extremely valuable. They can guide you to uncover issues blocking your energy flow. Just do an Internet search for "EFT Practitioner" in your local area.

Step 1: Identifying the Issue

When I saw an EFT practitioner, she guided me to look for the root cause(s) of the chronic eczema condition. Without treating the root cause(s), the symptoms would recur.

Ultimately, the skin infection was an expression of my deep fear for not being able to survive if I left my W-2 consulting job and followed my soul's calling to do REACH work. So, my fear of not being safe was one of the issues to release for my self-healing.

As another example, I mentioned earlier that I was really irritated when people did not respond to my emails. I was able to trace much of my triggered emotional response to a forgotten childhood wound of being ignored, that I did not count. So, I treated for energetic release of that emotional baggage.

Step 2: The Setup Statement

Next, I created the setup statement for use with tapping. This statement is intended to acknowledge the issue from Step 1, while accepting myself. So, my setup statements for the two examples above are: *"Even though I'm afraid I won't be able to take care of myself if I leave my livelihood, I deeply and profoundly accept myself,"* and *"Even though people ignore me and I don't count, I deeply and profoundly accept myself."*

This combination of acknowledging the issue with unconditional acceptance of myself is an important part of the treatment. Even though I am a big fan of affirmations, sometimes I feel like they can be too much of a stretch from where I am.

When I did research on EFT, I appreciated reading someone saying that, when he was dealing with a chronic illness, affirming that he was healthy, whole and complete simply did not feel genuine or believable to him. When we doubt whether something is believable, we know it simply will not work. So, the setup statement allows us to start with honoring where we are – by acknowledging the condition troubling us, while deeply and profoundly accepting ourselves – and go from there. It feels more genuine and real.

Step 3: The Tapping Sequence

Since the original EFT treatment protocol by Gary Craig, different variations have been developed and practiced. They have somewhat different tapping sequences, and they may incorporate other treatment components. I have tried three different variations, and they were all effective. They all included meridian points on the face, the collarbone, underarm and the karate chop point (see picture below).

The following tapping sequence is taken from www.TheTappingSolution.com. Do not worry about being precise with where you tap on these points. This technique is very forgiving.

- Karate chop – the fleshy part of the outer edge of your hand
- Eyebrow – the inner corner of your eyebrow where it meets your nose ridge
- Side of eye – the outer corner of your eye
- Under eye – the boney part of your eye socket under your eye
- Under nose – between your nose and upper lip
- Chin – the fleshy part of your chin
- Collarbone
- Under arm – about four inches under your armpit
- Top of head – crown of your head

Tapping Points

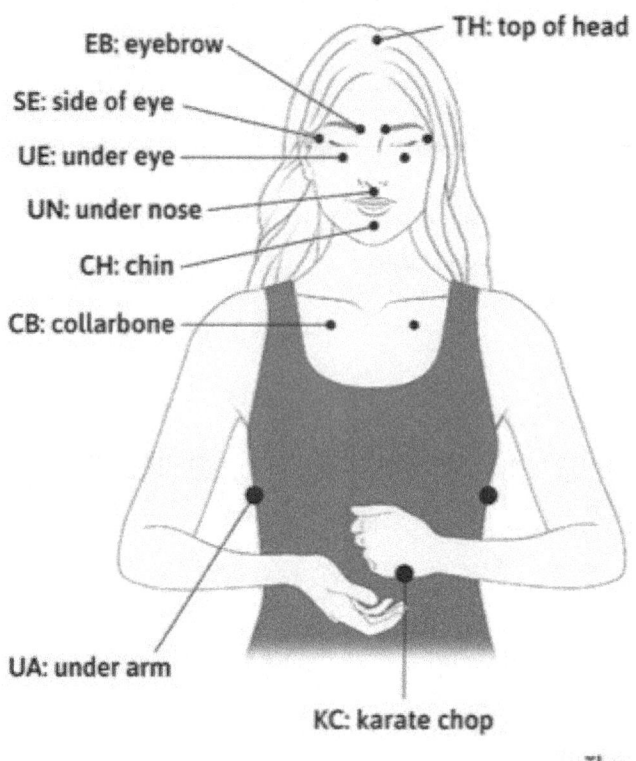

- TH: top of head
- EB: eyebrow
- SE: side of eye
- UE: under eye
- UN: under nose
- CH: chin
- CB: collarbone
- UA: under arm
- KC: karate chop

The Tapping Solution

To start, while tapping on my karate chop point, I said my setup statement three times. It did not have to be word for word each time, but the essence of the statements needed to be focused on the same issue.

On each subsequent meridian point, I tapped five to seven times with gentle but firm pressure. I used four fingers when tapping the wider areas, i.e., my head, under arm, collarbone and karate chop point, and two fingers – index and middle fingers – for the more delicate, smaller points on my face.

After tapping on my karate chop point with the setup statement, I continued to tap on the other points in the sequence. As I did so, I processed the emotions that came up, saying aloud what felt real to me about it.

About a month into my self-treatment, I got choked up when I simultaneously felt gratitude to my body for what it had endured and regret for having taken it all for granted. Similarly, as the childhood wound of feeling ignored and not counting emerged, I started sobbing.

This is the kind of emotional release we want with EFT. This is how the technique helps us release negative energy blockages. As I felt better about each issue, I was ready to consider better feeling thoughts and tap on those.

To illustrate with one of my examples above, one of my tapping sequences went something like this:

Karate Chop: *Even though I'm afraid I won't be able to take care of myself if I leave my livelihood, I deeply and profoundly accept myself. Even though I'm afraid I won't be able to take care of myself if I leave my livelihood, I deeply and profoundly accept myself. Even though I'm afraid I won't be able to take care of myself if I leave my livelihood, I deeply and profoundly accept myself.*

Eyebrow: *I just cannot quit my job.*

Side of eye: *It is what I know how to do well.*

Under eye: *It is how I pay my mortgage.*

Under nose: *It is how I have made a living for over 10 years.*

Chin: *What if I fall flat on my face?*

Collarbone:	*What if no one wants to read my book?*
Under arm:	*What if no one comes to my workshops?*
Top of head:	*I cannot walk away from financial security.*
Karate Chop:	*I guess I can keep my job while I finish my book.*
Eyebrow:	*I am self-employed, so I do have flexibility on when I work.*
Side of eye:	*Just focus on my intention for REACH.*
Under eye:	*I just want to help those who could benefit from REACH.*
Under nose:	*I had such a wonderful time teaching REACH Part One.*
Chin:	*I cannot wait for REACH Part Two!*
Collarbone:	*I am so happy when I am writing this book.*
Under arm:	*It is my life's work, and I love it!*
Top of head:	*I am following my calling. The universe won't leave me stranded.*

Step 4: Identifying the Intensity of the Condition

Most tapping resources suggest that we rate how we feel before and after tapping. For instance, on a scale of 0 to 10, we want to rate how intense or real the issue is to us before we tap, and again after we tap.

The idea is to gauge whether we feel improvement, and whether we want to tap some more. If I wanted to continue tapping on the above issue, I might have changed my setup statement to, "*Even though I am still afraid...*" That change in the setup statement acknowledges the improvement I felt, while continuing to seek further improvement.

With the eczema condition, I had a lot of big fears and beliefs that were trapped. For instance, even as my condition started improving, I was hesitant to allow myself to eat the "forbidden foods" that triggered an allergic response. That was because the fear of eating the wrong things was so strong, and the belief had been with me for so long, that it was challenging to release them in one or two rounds of tapping.

That was why it took a few months for me to heal myself. As I released my fears over time, though, I started to open up to the possibility of alternative possibilities. My belief about the condition shifted eventually, and my mind was trained to look for supporting evidence for the new belief. I gradually started eating things I could not eat before.

As you can see, EFT is a very simple technique. It has produced powerful results for many, including for me. Because it honors where we are emotionally about the condition troubling us, it allows us to acknowledge and accept it without pushing against it or trying to suppress it. As such, this technique is less likely to elicit an undercurrent of resistance within us, thereby allowing our bodies to relax and gradually let go of the trapped negative energy. This is why it is great for working with big fears that may take a little time to process and dissolve progressively.

The Power of Forgiveness

Any discussion of releasing negativity is incomplete without forgiveness. Forgiveness is important because resentment, anger and bitterness all take up precious room in our creative space and block our good from coming into our lives.

If we find it challenging to imagine ourselves in the life of our dreams, that is a good indicator that there are emotional toxins blocking our energy flow. Perhaps, we are still caught up in the bitterness of an on-going trying circumstance, or we may still be hanging onto residual anger toward someone or something. It is critical to let these emotional toxins go.

When we practice forgiveness, we release judgment of ourselves and others. Instead, we allow ourselves to learn to accept those experiences that hurt us. It may take some time in the case of particularly traumatic events – I know this first-hand.

However, it is well worth the effort to clear your space of the emotional remnants of the trauma. Think about it when you dwell on the hurt, anger, resentment or bitterness about a wrong done to you. Does the offender get affected by your feelings? Does feeling this way make the wrong any more palatable? Can feeling this way rewrite history and save you from having to experience it in the first place?

Quite simply, ask yourself this one question: *What do I gain by hanging onto these hurtful feelings?*

Please understand that what I am advocating here is not for us to go into denial about what happened. Having survived several traumatic experiences in my life, I will never make light of how real and debilitating some life challenges can be.

Letting go of hurt is not the same thing as grieving. When we grieve our losses, we give ourselves the time and space to acknowledge what happened and to honor the feelings of loss, allowing them to run their natural course. There is no way around painful experiences but to go through them. They are part of the human experience. However, we also need to allow healing to take place over time. And, at some point, when healing has run its course, it would be time to let the grievance go.

We will never forget what happened. But, if we allow complete healing to occur, the emotional charge associated with the event will dissolve in time. We will be able to make peace with the experience and gain perspective on it. And, if we are willing, we can even experience a personal breakthrough as a result of living through the pain.

I definitely have been blessed with profound breakthroughs from my own traumatic experiences.

For a great, inspiring story of gaining appreciation from trauma, read Rosemary's Story in *Love for no Reason* by Marci Shimoff. Rosemary is a rape survivor. While, as she said, she would never have chosen to be raped, she was able to recognize in time how that experience expanded her compassionate heart, how it deepened her faith that she was loved and supported even through the most egregious violation a woman could suffer.

If a rape survivor could let go of her emotional baggage, couldn't we all learn to let our grievance stories go? Again, it may take time, conscious effort and courage. But do you really want to go through life with a constricted heart and tense body, constantly scraping by in survival mode? You can have so much more by making room for good to come to you.

As Louise Hay wrote in *You Can Heal Your Life*, we do not need to know *how* to forgive, nor does it mean we have to condone the harmful behavior of others. Just by being *willing* to forgive, we are open to releasing that part of us that feels anger or hurt when we think of the person or the situation that hurt us.

By being willing to forgive, we choose to tend to our own well being. It has nothing to do with the offending party or circumstances. It is simply our own commitment to let go of what hurts us inside, which ultimately only traps *us* in our own internal suffering. So, be willing to break down the walls of that internal prison and welcome freedom.

It is also important to forgive because it prevents us from recreating the same negative conditions in a new setting. As a case in point, after the life-altering accident at the end of 2008, I spent months to prepare psychologically to leave my job to become self-employed. Part of the preparation included practicing forgiveness (and gratitude).

Alice P. Chan, Ph.D.

At the time, I had accumulated a full load of anger and resentment toward my employer. I knew that if I did not spend the time to forgive the owners – and myself for not having the courage to leave sooner – I would only recreate the same negative conditions in my own consulting business. That is, I would again feel over-worked, under-paid and under-appreciated, as well as powerless to choose a better situation for myself.

By the time I felt ready to give notice, I was much more at peace and ready to close that chapter of my life and start a new one. I did not want to leave the owners and my team in a lurch. Instead, I decided to give a six-week notice, so that they could have time to prepare for my departure accordingly.

On the day that I sat down to write my resignation letter, I wanted to communicate from the highest part of myself. I meditated and set my intention to speak only from a place of gratitude for what that job had enabled me to do, and what I had learned in the four-plus years I was with that company.

I had spent months writing list upon list of things I needed to forgive and things for which I was grateful. By the time I wrote that resignation letter, I had released the anger and bitterness but retained the reasons to be grateful.

During the time that I meditated and focused on this letter, a very interesting thing happened. The senior vice president from a company at which I had interviewed twice in the year and a half prior contacted me out of the blue. She wanted to find out if I would be open to talking with her again. To make a long story short, one thing led to another, and I was offered a vice president position.

For years, it had been my dream to reach that level in my career by the time I turned 40. That offer came seven months before my 40th birthday. Even though I ended up turning down the job, I did thank the universe for showing me that I could have lived that dream, if I still wanted it.

I share the above story to illustrate the amazing power of forgiveness. Is it a coincidence that the same company passed on me for the same position twice before, only to want me again when I had done my forgiveness and gratitude work? I think not.

As Dr. Deepak Chopra teaches very eloquently in *The Spontaneous Fulfillment of Desires*, there is no such thing as coincidence in life. What appears as coincidence is really synchronicity – when seemingly random events with matching energies occur simultaneously.

Remember the radio receiver metaphor? When our thoughts, feelings and beliefs are on the same frequencies as our desires, the latter manifest in our lives – even if in the form of seeming coincidences. When I emptied my anger bag and installed gratitude-based messages in my consciousness, I changed the tuner on my radio to receive the vice president position. The offer materialized because I had finally cleared the path for it to come into my life.

O *Contemplation Exercise*

- Who do you need to forgive and for what?
- In what ways may you need to forgive yourself? Give this question careful consideration, especially if you have a tendency to be hard on yourself.

Forgiveness is such a high priority that it is ascribed by Edwene Gaines as one of the laws in *The Four Spiritual Laws of Prosperity*. She recommends that we ask ourselves every night before we go to sleep whether we have put anyone outside of our hearts that day.

She also advocates that we do a thorough forgiveness inventory once a year. We want to think of everyone we know and everything we have experienced in the year and check in to see if we have any lingering resentment, anger or other residual ill feelings toward any of them. Again, whether you choose to follow her precise advice, it is critical that forgiveness is part of your on-going REACH practice.

Congratulations on all the great work you have done to uncover and release old beliefs and barriers to your dreams! From my own personal experience, I know this takes courage, tenacity and devotion. You should be really proud of your willingness to clear your creative space for a better version of your life.

The tools in this chapter will always be here if and when you need to revisit any of them at any point as you REACH your dreams. For now, treat yourself to something to celebrate what you have done in this chapter. It will signal to your subconscious that you are making great progress in shifting your consciousness to welcome your dreams. We will talk more about this in Chapter 5 - Celebrate. Meanwhile, go celebrate!

Summary Points for Release

- ❖ Fears and old beliefs block our path to our dreams. Therefore, we need to identify and release them.

- ❖ Messages we carry with us, guiding us how to act and how to make decisions are often not our truth, but what we internalized from our childhood experiences. When we notice such a message emerging, ask, *"Whose line is it anyway? Who am I trying to honor? Does it really serve me now and where I want to go?"*

- ❖ Pay attention to where you focus your time and energy. Whether the dominant themes are positive or negative tells you what energy *you* project that attracts people and events to mirror back to you the beliefs, perspective and outlook *you* offer.

- ❖ Pay attention to what pushes your buttons, and what life patterns you have been unknowingly repeating. What irritates you tells you about judgments you have that are trying to get your attention to be released. Similarly, the painful life patterns you repeat are also reflections of unhealed wounds that are surfacing to be healed.

- ❖ What you try to avoid is associated with the fears your soul knows you are ready to release, because you are ready to grow. Ignoring these nudges might eventually draw in harsher wakeup calls in the form of illnesses or accidents to get your attention. Your subconscious mind thinks it is buying you time to avoid doing what you need to do, but your soul knows that overcoming your fears is in your best interest.

- ❖ Repeat the Treasure Chest Meditation, as needed, to uncover, release and update old agreements and promises you made with yourself in the past that no longer serve you.

Alice P. Chan, Ph.D.

- ❖ Challenge the barriers you feel are on your path to your dreams. Are they really true?

- ❖ Find a release ritual that resonates with you to signal clearly that you are done with the old beliefs that come up to be released.

- ❖ With Emotional Freedom Technique (EFT), we can tap our way out of fears and limiting beliefs blocking our dreams and into new affirming beliefs aligned with where we want to go.

- ❖ EFT honors where we are and what we are ready to do. It allows us to consciously detach from a tenacious limiting belief and work progressively on letting it go. Learn more about this technique, and look for a certified practitioner in your area.

- ❖ Forgiveness releases emotional toxins taking up valuable room in your creative space, and prevents the re-creation of the same undesirable conditions in another setting. Therefore, releasing anger, bitterness and resentment is key to clearing your path to your dreams.

CHAPTER 3

Envision

"Each of us has an inner dream that we can unfold if we will just have the courage to admit what it is. And the faith to trust our own admission."
— Julia Cameron

You may have read and worked with the tools in *The Artist's Way: A Spiritual Path to Higher Creativity* by Julia Cameron. To me, whether or not we actually consider ourselves artists, all of us are born with some form of creativity within us. It could be something readily recognizable as creative, such as painting/drawing or sculpting. It could also be something less obvious, such as creative problem solving or an innate ease of making connections across abstract ideas.

Regardless of its specific form, our creativity yearns to be awakened and expressed. What's more, we can really engage this part of ourselves to compose the life of our dreams. More importantly, as Cameron said in the above quote, each of us has an inner dream waiting to unfold – waiting for us to *allow* it to unfold. We unknowingly disallow it from happening by being too caught up in the busyness of our daily lives to pay attention. We block the unfolding with latent fear about what knowing this inner dream would mean, that it may nudge us to leave our comfort zone.

Through what she calls "Morning Pages," she encourages us to write three pages longhand first thing every morning to allow anything and everything that crosses our mind to be revealed. This advice makes perfect sense to me. After all, with such unabridged stream of consciousness, great ideas can flow from the most creative part of ourselves. They are the creative impulses that are often drowned out – by the vast amount of mental chatter going on most of the time and any self-talk we may have about not being creative.

That is why it is good to do this unstructured creative download first thing in the morning. We are still fresh, and our capacities have yet to be taken up by the demands we feel from our everyday life responsibilities. The busyness of our day has yet to power up fully to suppress the creative impulses trying to get our attention from deep within us.

By giving our inner creator some airtime each day, we give ourselves the opportunity to get to know who we really are and what we truly desire. This can be done without feeling like we have to overhaul our lives abruptly to choose something completely different from what we know.

Whether or not you decide to write Morning Pages specifically, the idea of letting our inner dream unfold is the essence of what *envisioning* is all about. In particular, rather than looking outside of ourselves to define what we want, to seek what we think or feel will make us happy, the real life of our dreams is an inner vision to be awakened.

If you think about why you picked up this book, it is likely because you have felt an *inner* stirring to do something about your life, isn't it? Even if you want to improve the external circumstances of your life, the nudging you feel to do something about your life typically comes from within.

In the last chapter, we did quite a bit of internal housecleaning to make room in our creative space for our dreams. Our next task at hand is to get clear about what we want. Therefore, in this chapter, we will continue our journey inward, but this time for the purpose of awakening our juicy inner dream.

Are you ready for this delicious task? We will discuss ways to allow our inner vision to come forward, so that we can see and, more importantly, feel ourselves living in the desired conditions. I will start with two of my favorite meditations for envisioning. I encourage you to practice them periodically, as they are very powerful. We will also talk about doing visualizations in different ways. When you have a clear picture of what you want, feeling your dreams as if they have already manifested is great fun!

Visioning Meditation

The first envisioning tool I want to introduce to you is that of a visioning meditation. Visioning is not to be confused with visualization, which we will cover later in this chapter. Even though visioning sounds similar to visualizing, these two are different concepts and come with different processes.

Unlike visualization in which we *choose* the conditions we want, visioning is about letting the conditions that are for our highest good come to us. Visioning is not driven by our rational mind, even though the outcomes will be pleasant to it as well – whether it is more abundance, a better career, a great romantic partnership or better health. When we engage in visioning, we ask our ever-responsible ego to take a nap, while we invite our inner wisdom and creativity to come forward and talk to us.

We engage our Yin energy in visioning through meditation. By getting into a meditative state, we close our eyes and consciously cease attention to mind chatter for the duration of the meditation. In doing so, we create a special space that is free of distraction or any desire to control our environment. In this space, we open ourselves to seeing, hearing, feeling and/or knowing the qualities of the inner dream awaiting our attention.

We let the wisest and most creative part of ourselves reveal a better, more satisfying version of life to us. This part of us is not bogged down by any lingering fears, worries or limiting beliefs. From this fearless place of creation, we allow the picture of the best version of our dream to be revealed to us.

To engage in visioning, the meditation I practice follows what was created by Rev. Dr. Michael Beckwith of the Agape International Spiritual Center. It consists of the following questions:

1. What is [my best and most creative self's] highest vision for _____?
2. What do I need to release or let go of for this vision to be realized?
3. What do I need to embrace or become for this vision to be realized?
4. What else do I need to know?

The blank in the first question is the subject of your visioning, e.g., your life, your dream relationship, the next steps regarding your career, and so forth. Depending on your spiritual beliefs, this question could be posed to the Higher Power of your understanding, such as "God," "Spirit," "Source," "Providence," etc. That is why "my best and most creative self's" is enclosed in brackets; you can customize it to whomever is most salient to you.

When I did my visioning meditation on New Year's Eve, for instance, my question was: *What is the Divine's highest vision for me in 2011?* One answer I got is one of my guiding principles for the year, which I mentioned in the Prologue: *Love awaits harvesting in your heart.*

It really does not matter what you call this Higher Power, or whether you even believe in one. When you get into this receptive, meditative state, this question is posed to the highest, most fearless part of you. That is why you will likely get more than what your ego could conjure up.

The subsequent three questions are intended to provide you with more guidance on what to do to realize the vision just revealed to you. With the second question, *"What do I need to release or let go of for this vision to be realized,"* it will reveal to you what no longer serves you, the roadblocks to be cleared on your path. These blocks could be fears, latent anger about something or someone, needs for forgiveness, judgment of self and others, and so on. You can use the tools from the *Release* chapter to clear whatever is revealed to you to be released.

Meanwhile, with the third question, *"What do I need to embrace or become for this vision to be realized,"* you will receive insights on how you may need to grow, perhaps by learning something new, or taking action in some other way that propels you forward.

As an example, for my New Year's Eve meditation, one of the insights from asking this question was my other 2011 guiding principle: *Become the best version of you.*

With the final "what else" question, we ask for any additional insights there may be. When I did my very first visioning meditation to ask about the highest vision for my life a few years ago, the first response I got to the last question was: *Have fun!* It was very unexpected, after all the serious insights revealed to me earlier in the meditation. The surprise of this message made it more real and believable to me, as I knew my rational mind did not come up with it.

In this visioning meditation, answers may come to you in the form of words, images, feelings, or just a sense of knowing. You may get insights in any of these forms, or you may consistently get only one form.

For me, I mostly see words or hear messages. Sometimes, I get images as well, and occasionally I would also feel vivid sensations while being part of a visual picture shown to me. So, when you engage in visioning, be prepared to take note of the insights by writing or drawing. You may not have words for what comes to you. That is perfectly valid. Trust the message that comes in whatever form from deep within you.

As shown in my example above, when you get insights that surprise you, it is actually a very good sign that it is something truly coming from the wisest, more fearless part of you, rather than from your rational mind or ego.

A few years back, when I was new to conscious living tools and trying to build a spiritual practice, I would begin almost every morning with a visioning meditation for the day. I would start the sequence of questions with: *What is the Divine's highest vision for my day?* I wanted to be in the right frame of mind for the day.

Before long, I learned to tune into my internal guidance system, including warnings. That is, when I got distinct messages about embracing peace, harmony or the like, I knew to be prepared for things happening for which it would be up to me to *choose* not to react negatively.

On one Friday, when I did this visioning meditation, I was told to embrace spontaneity and remain flexible. Within hours, my entire work day and weekend were turned completely upside down. People needed to cancel plans and/or wanted to reschedule, and unexpected things showed up that required my immediate attention.

As an organized planner, having so much chaos unraveling in a short amount of time would normally have created a lot of stress for me. However, my visioning meditation earlier that morning prepared me to be conscious of *choosing* to roll with the punches. In the end, everything and everyone needing my attention got it, even if not in the order of the original plan.

REACH Your Dreams

In short, this visioning process is powerful not just for big questions related to awakening your inner dream. It can also be a very useful tool to help you stay conscious of your choices in day-to-day living. We will talk more about taking action on visioning in the next chapter, *Act*.

Meanwhile, give this really simple but powerful visioning meditation a try. Be open to welcoming whatever insights that may come to you. You may very well be surprised by the immense wisdom you have within you all along, waiting for you to pay attention.

O *Meditation Exercise*

If this is the first time you are doing this meditation, you may want to ask for insights on the highest vision for your life. This will give you the big picture of your life within which your dream is a part. However, if you would prefer to ask specifically about your dream, please do so.

Have your journal or workbook ready. Stop after each question to jot down what comes to you. When you are ready to move on to the next question, just take a few deep breaths and resume the meditation with the next question.

- Close your eyes, and take several slow, deep breaths. With each breath in, imagine your body being gradually filled up with the most powerful, cleansing energy. With each breath out, feel your body releasing any tension, stress or discomfort. Repeat this breathing until you feel relaxed and grounded, and your mind is quiet.

- What is [my best and most creative self's] highest vision for my life/dream?

- What do I need to release or let go of for this vision to be realized?

- What do I need to embrace or become for this vision to be realized?

- What else do I need to know?

When you are done with the meditation, journal on what came up for you. What overall themes emerged for you? What do you need to embrace and let go of to realize this vision? What, if anything, surprises you? How so?

Remember, even if you do not yet understand their meaning, surprises are good signs that these insights came from your wise inner knowing, not your rational mind. It is good to do this meditation periodically to check in for any new insights.

Chakra Meditation

As a second envisioning tool, we will be seeking insights from different energy centers within our body, which constantly radiates and receives energy. There are many energy centers in our body that are associated with different purposes. For instance, in the *Release* chapter, I told you about how I tapped on a series of energy points on my hand, face, upper body and head with Emotional Freedom Technique to release trapped negative energy.

Aside from those meridian points, there are seven energy centers running parallel to our spine – from its base to the top of our head – that are associated with our different needs and desires, such as financial security, love, and so on. These energy centers are referred to as *chakras*, the Sanskrit word for "wheel," to connote wheel-like energy vortices in our body.

By tuning into each of these seven energy centers, we can tap into insights about different parts of our dream, including potential barriers to its realization, as they relate to meeting different levels of our needs and desires.

Whether or not these energy centers are open – allowing clear energy to flow – is affected by the quality of our thoughts and feelings. When we feel grounded, secure and optimistic, the energy is clear and bright.

The energy whirling in each chakra is of a different color. The clarity and vibrancy of the color reflects the state of our consciousness and whether there is fear – known or unknown – trapped in our body.

When we are in fear about something, whether it is related to survival or higher-level desires, the associated energy center becomes blocked, and the energy trapped is dirty and cloudy, thereby obscuring the healthy color of the chakra. When this happens, we need to clear these blockages before we can access our inner wisdom.

There is an abundance of resources available on the Web and in published books, if you are interested in learning more about the seven chakras.

For our purposes, let me quickly introduce you to each of these seven powerful energy vortices and their associated life issues. Then, I will outline for you a chakra meditation I have practiced regularly for a few years. It was one of the meditations I did on New Year's Eve 2010 that yielded great insights.

This is a great meditation for accessing your inner wisdom about different aspects of your dream, and what actions you may need to take to realize your dream.

1. **Root Chakra** – This energy center is located at the base of our spine. It is associated with thoughts and feelings about money, safety and security. In other words, this energy center has to do with our survival needs and feelings of physical and emotional safety, as well as financial security. When healthy and unblocked

by fears, worries or limiting beliefs, the energy whirling in this chakra has a bright ruby red color.

2. **Sacral Chakra** – This is located in our abdomen, about four inches above our root chakra, midway between our naval and the base of our spine. This energy center is associated with our desires and appetite for life, as well as feelings about our bodies, including health and physical appearance. When we do not feel that our desires are met, are afraid to go after what we want in life, or have issues with our health or weight, this chakra is blocked. When healthy, the color of this energy vortex is a bright orange.

3. **Solar Plexus Chakra** – This is in our stomach area, right behind our navel, and the energy center associated with power and control. When this energy center is clear and strong, we feel we are in integrity with what we do and say. When we blame or feel like a victim, this energy center is blocked, and we give our personal power away, by allowing someone else or external circumstances to control us. When healthy, our Solar Plexus glows with a yellow color, like a little sun right in our stomach.

4. **Heart Chakra** – As you might guess, this is the energy center associated with our ability to give and receive love. Located in our chest, this chakra reflects our thoughts and feelings about relationships in our lives and any emotional attachments we have to people. This is also where we hold our ability to accept and love ourselves. When our heart chakra is healthy, it radiates a beautiful emerald green color.

5. **Throat Chakra** – This is the energy center associated with speaking our truth, asking for what we need, and not being afraid of changes in our lives. When we are fearful of communicating in anyway, such as feeling we are under a gag order, this energy center is blocked. When the throat chakra is open and clear, it has a pretty light blue color.

6. **Third Eye Chakra** – It is located between our eyes, and is associated with our willingness and ability to see the truth and the future. When we are free of fears or disbelief about seeing our truth or future, this energy wheel shows a dark blue color; it may appear as an oval shape in your meditation, just like an eye.

7. **Crown Chakra** – It is located at the top of our head, and is the energy center associated with our connection to cosmic wisdom, our sense of knowingness. When we feel tuned into the energy of the universe, we receive guidance that is not tied to any fears or worries in our daily lives, even if the information is related to our life circumstances. When this energy center is clear, it is purple in col

O *Meditation Exercise*

Now that you have a basic introduction to the seven chakras, you are ready to go into meditation. In each energy center:

- You will first see or feel the color of that energy center.

- Notice if there are any dark spots, which represent latent fears, worries or limiting beliefs. If there is darkness, you will clear the blockages.

- Following the cleansing, you will affirm your truth associated with that particular chakra.

- Then, you will pose a question about your life or your dream, e.g., *What do I need to know about my dream?*

- If you see, hear or feel something you don't understand, ask: *Why am I seeing/hearing/feeling this?*

This is a rather long meditation, so you may want to tape record the different steps to guide yourself through it. Also, allow at least 20 minutes to complete the meditation itself and another 10 to 15 minutes to process what you will have received. Have your journal or workbook close by to jot down insights from each chakra. Again, be prepared to draw, as images or feelings instead of words may come to you.

- Close your eyes, and take several slow, deep breaths. With each breath in, imagine your body being gradually filled up with the most powerful, cleansing energy. With each breath out, feel your body releasing any tension, stress or discomfort. Repeat this breathing until you feel relaxed and grounded, and your mind is quiet.

- Place your attention on the base of your spine, your Root Chakra.
    - See or feel a ruby red circle.
    - Notice if there are any dark spots, which represent fears, worries and other negative blockages. If so, ask the higher power of your understanding or the wisest and most loving part of you to cleanse away this darkness.
    - Then, affirm: *My needs are already met. I am safe, and I am secure.*
    - Now, ask your question: *What do I need to know about my dream?*
    - If you don't know why this information is revealed to you, gently ask: *Why am I seeing/feeling/hearing this?*

- Now, move your attention about four inches up to the area between your root chakra and your navel. This is your Sacral Chakra.
    - See or feel an orange circle.

- Again, ask your higher power or your inner wisdom and love to cleanse away any darkness you see.
- Then, affirm: *My desires are aligned with the ceaseless universal flow of supplies.*
- Ask your question, and see, hear or feel any insight.
- As needed, ask, "*Why am I seeing/feeling/hearing this?*"

- Next, move up to your stomach area, right behind your navel. This is your Solar Plexus.
  - See or feel a bright yellow circle, like a brilliant little sun sitting right in your tummy.
  - Repeat the cleansing step above, and then affirm: *I fearlessly activate my personal power to serve.*
  - Ask this energy center your question, and seek clarification, as needed.

- Moving up to your chest, this is your Heart Chakra.
  - See or feel an emerald green circle.
  - Repeat all of the above steps, and use the following affirmation: *I fearlessly give and receive love.*

- Onto your Throat Chakra,
  - See or feel a light blue circle.
  - Repeat all of the above steps, and use the following affirmation: *I fearlessly speak my truth.*

- Now, focus your attention in the area between your eyes. This is your Third Eye.
  - See or feel a dark blue oval shape, which could literally look like an eye.

- Repeat all of the above steps, and use the following affirmation: *I fearlessly see the future and my truth.*

- Finally, focus on the top of your head just inside your skull. This is your Crown Chakra.
  - See or feel a purple circle.
  - Repeat all of the above steps, and use the following affirmation: *I listen, I trust and I take guided action.*

Take a moment to review the insights that came to you and journal on them. What, if anything, really jumped out at you? What did you see that did not immediately make sense to you? The message, "*Finish REACH book. Just do it. You have a message to share. Don't delay,*" came to me in my Throat Chakra when I meditated. Quite the ultimate message of urging me to speak my truth!

With the above two meditations, you now have two very powerful envisioning tools for tapping into your inner dream. You probably got some juicy insights on next steps already. We will talk about taking action on them in the next chapter.

As you make progress toward your dream, repeat these meditations periodically to check in for possible new insights. Also, these meditations are great tools for accessing your inner wisdom for any question or issue you may be facing, not just to get clarity on your inner dream. They are powerful ways to go beyond the limits of your rational mind to come up with creative insights.

Visualization

Most of what you may have heard or read about manifestations involves the process of visualization. It is a powerful way to imagine your dreams into reality, especially when you have a clear idea of what you want.

With visualization, the idea is what the late Dr. Wayne Dyer urged us to do in *The Power of Intention*: Contemplate yourself being surrounded by the conditions you want. That is, literally picture yourself looking around you at the conditions of having already manifested your dreams – from the perspective of being *in* these conditions. If you are looking from the outside at yourself in the picture, you are not *in* it.

Beyond seeing, the more important part is to *feel* what it is like to be in those conditions. In *The Secret*, there is a scene with a man sitting in his recliner at home, imagining himself driving the sports car of his dream. He imagines himself pressing on the gas paddle, feeling the G-force of the fast car in motion, and hearing the roaring engine – all as if he truly is driving this car.

Similarly, a friend of mine says that, when she visualizes herself in a new job, she not only sees herself driving to the new office. She literally feels her work clothes on her skin, as she is tugged in the driver seat of her car. She visualizes the entire experience with her five senses. She is a former competitive athlete, and visualization was a regular part of her preparation for competition.

The key with visualization is to feel the experience as if it is real, not just a concoction of your imagination.

When people say that visualization does not work, often one of the key missing links is the feeling part (the other is not taking action). Our subconscious mind cannot distinguish between what is an actual vs. an imagined experience, if it feels real. When we can actually feel the tangible and tactile experience of having something – like in a real-life experience – having this thing registers as a belief.

This is the whole point of doing visualizations – to train our subconscious to believe that what we visualize is real and that it is ours to have. Otherwise, our radio receiver is not tuned into receiving it. And, the visualization itself would merely be a series of pleasant pictures consisting of thoughts that come and go without any staying power.

In short, visualization – powered by the accompanying feelings of having your desires met – broadcasts clear signals at frequencies that call in matching experiences. Again, when you genuinely believe in something, by universal law, the external circumstances of your life *must* line up to match your internal state.

Let me give you a detailed example from my personal experience to illustrate this process. I will point out the key components of my visualization which manifested the experience in real life.

After the unpleasant way 2008 ended, I wanted to go into the year-end holidays of 2009 with gratitude and positive expectancy. Furthermore, the holidays have always struck a sentimental chord in me, and inspired me to think of romance.

So, on one autumn day in 2009, I sat down to visualize the upcoming Christmas with a romantic partner. At the time, I was single, not dating anyone, nor even trying to meet anyone. After all, my primary focus was on preparing to transition into self-employment. As such, there was no one particular in mind when I did the visualization.

I closed my eyes, and started letting the screenplay of my imagination take over. I was in my softly lit living room, sitting on my couch next to someone whose arm was around me. There was a lovely feeling of tenderness enveloping us. I saw my Christmas tree (even though I had yet to put it up in reality), sparkling in a magical way with the ornaments I loved. One of my favorite Christmas songs – "*Christmas by the Bay*" by Tim Huckleberry – was playing in the background, as we sipped on delicious sparkling cider.

It was a very cozy and romantic scene. For a few minutes, I just allowed myself to be swept up in the sweetness of this wonderful experience. Everything was as real as if it all actually happened – and I was simply recalling a pleasant memory – rather than it being the product of my imagination.

When I was done, I went back to my life in progress, not giving it another thought. Before long, I had forgotten all about that visualization.

Two weeks before Christmas, I met a man without even trying. On New Year's Eve, we went dancing, and had a truly romantic time. When the dance ended, we went back to my house to spend more time together. I popped open a bottle of sparkling cider for the occasion. My date was curious about my music collection, and wanted me to play some of my favorite songs for him.

I proceeded to play a number of them, including "*Christmas by the Bay.*" That CD was still sitting on top of one of the speakers; I had not put it away since I last played it over Christmas. I remember saying to him that it was not Christmas anymore. However, he said that my tree was still up, and the ambiance was just right.

So, I pressed play on the CD player, and went back to the couch where he was sitting. He put his arm around me, as Tim serenaded us. At that very moment, it hit me that I was in the precise scene with the precise visuals, sounds, smells, tastes and feelings I had visualized a couple of months earlier!

As you can clearly see, when done with all the right components, visualization really works! My experience above is just one example. Note that all it took was a single seating for me to visualize that romantic experience into reality.

My visualization registered as real because I truly felt it, and my subconscious mind believed it. It did not know that the scene was something I imagined, instead of an experience that actually happened. It only took cues from how I felt, along with the details of what I saw, heard, tasted and smelled, none of which contained any shred of doubt about the realness of the experience. So, my belief that this imagined scenario was real got released to the universe to work its magic. In turn, the right circumstances lined up to match the frequencies I offered through my visualization exercise.

If I was not entirely comfortable with the scene I imagined, or if a part of me was stuck in the consciousness that I was not dating anyone at the time of my visualization, that I did not have a clue as to who would actually fulfill that scene with me, it would not have worked. In other words, the *absence* of the conditions could not be the point from which to attract the experience.

Again, it is what you believe that sets your radio tuner to receive the experience. Notice that, in my story above, I did not see myself being whisked off in style to Monte Carlo by a handsome prince. That would have been too far-fetched for me to believe – nor would I have wanted it, really. Instead, I pictured myself in a very familiar environment (my home) in a scenario with realistic components (e.g., my tree, music, sparkling cider, etc.). The only stretch was that I did not know who would be sharing that experience with me. That stretch did not trigger any doubts or disbelief, and so the entire experience felt real and believable to my subconscious mind.

Besides choosing something realistic in which I could believe, another reason why my visualization worked is because I had no attachment to the scenario, even though I desired it and felt it vividly. What I mean by attachment is that I did not feel my happiness would hinge on this event happening. While the manifestation of this desire would indeed be a great gift to grace the Holidays, it would not ruin Christmas for me if this never happened.

I simply released what I visualized, trusted that the request had been received, and went on with my life. I did not obsess about it, which would have told my subconscious inadvertently that what I visualized was not real, but just my imagination of something I really wanted.

REACH Your Dreams

To summarize from my detailed example above, below are the key components of effective visualization:

- Picture yourself *in* the experience looking around at the conditions you want, instead of looking at the picture and seeing yourself in it as an outsider.

- Really *feel* the experience. Engage as many of your senses as possible.

- Make it as real as you can, so that your subconscious mind believes that it is real.

- Repeat the visualization only to the extent that it will help you believe in the experience. Do not repeat if it might remind you of the current absence of what you want, or if it might activate latent doubts about whether you can actually have it – whether you *deserve* to have it.

- Choose a scenario that you actually believe can happen. If it is too much of a stretch from where you are, you will have a hard time believing that it can come true.

- Really enjoy the experience, and then detach from the outcome. That is, don't obsess about it, or feel that it would be devastating if it did not happen. Otherwise, you risk activating the feelings of not having it, which contradicts the scene you will have just tried to register with your subconscious as being real. The absence of what you desire cannot be the point of attraction for what you want.

If you are new to visualization, practice first with something small, such as finding a parking space. This may sound like a cliché of an example. However, that is actually a good place to start, so that you can build some experience and confidence in the process.

If you have doubts about whether you can truly visualize your dream into reality, these doubts will work against the process. Therefore, even though your dream is ultimately what you want – whether a new relationship, a new job or some other significant life change – I would recommend against starting immediately with such a big desire to which you probably have considerable attachment and expectations. Again, to recognize if you are emotionally attached to something, check in with yourself to see if your happiness and well-being is heavily dependent on its manifestation.

O *Visualization Exercise*

- Think of something you want that you genuinely believe is attainable, even if it is a stretch in some way.

- Depending on how big this desire is, spend 5 to 10 minutes visualizing being in the conditions of already having it. Engage as many of your senses as possible. Though it is not necessary, you may find it helpful to outline the conditions of what you want first before doing the visualization with these elements in mind.

- When you are done, let it go, and get on with your life.

When you get results, journal about them. Repeat this exercise, increasing the "bigness" of your desire as you feel ready. Be sure to keep track of your wins with your visualizations. It will help you build confidence in your natural abilities to manifest your own life experiences, however small they may be to begin. Big or small, the same process and principles apply.

Fun Visualization Tools: Vision Board, Scrapbook and Magic Box

If you find the above visualization exercise a little too abstract for you, and would prefer something more tactile, there are other tools you can use. They are really fun, and are great ways to get your creative juices going, while engaging good-feeling thoughts. *How* you visualize is less important than making sure that the key elements of effective visualization – listed in the above section – are incorporated. You want whatever tool you use to keep you feeling good about your desires, to help you believe that your dream is attainable, and to induce every fiber of your being to feel how real the experience is.

Vision Board. As a fun visualization tool, create a vision board. What you need is a poster board, which you can get inexpensively at any craft store, and a bunch of magazines from which you can clip pictures. The poster board will serve as your blank canvas for creating the collage of your dream life or one particular dream, e.g., a new job, a new relationship, a new home, etc.

As you flip through different magazines and see pictures representing the conditions you desire, clip them, and paste them on your vision board. Arrange these cutouts anyway you want. It is *your* vision. Feel free to add your own drawings and/or other items that symbolize the dream you would like to create.

As an example, in *The Secret*, one of the contributors, John Assaraf, talks about living in the precise house he had on his vision board a few years prior. He had forgotten about doing that – he had detached from the vision once it was offered.

Similarly, a big item on my vision board created a few years back came true last year: I went on my dream Mediterranean cruise to celebrate my 40th birthday. Specifically, I got to spend my actual birthday on Santorini, which thrilled me to no end! And, for 12 days, I ate well, had tons of fun visiting various Greek Isles, Ephesus (Turkey), the Amalfi Coast of Italy and Venice, and had not a care in the world.

Scrapbook. A similar idea to a vision board is scrapbooking. Just like collecting pictures and symbols of events that have already taken place, you will be gathering artifacts of what your dream would look like, as if it already manifested.

In the audio program, *Infinite Possibilities*, Mike Dooley from Totally Unique Things (www.tut.com), talked about his experience of collecting pictures of places around the world he wanted to visit. One day, as he was having breakfast in his hotel in Hong Kong, the scene he was looking at was precisely one of the pictures he had in his scrapbook. Imagine how uncanny, but fun, that experience of manifestation must have been!

Magic Box. Still another fun way to visualize is through a magic box. This idea is from the book, *Ask And It Is Given* by Jerry and Esther Hicks. This box can be of any size, shape, material and construction.

The important part is to have fun with it, decorate it, and make it truly something magical to you. In the magic box, you put items representing what you want to manifest, much like you would collect pictures and artifacts for a vision board or a scrapbook. However, since you are working with a box, you can include larger items that may not easily fit on a poster board or in a scrapbook.

At a weekend workshop a few years ago, I created my magic box that ended up looking like a little girl's lunchbox. I guess my inner creativity wanted a reminder of what it is like to be a child again – the unbounded, uncensored creative expression and the desire to have fun.

Even though this box is not my primary envisioning and manifestation tool, I have had fun putting things in it over time that reflect my desires. One of the wishes I had put in my magic box a few years ago was to play tennis with fun people two to three times a week at a health club I had just joined. At the time, I did not know anyone there, and it was more challenging to meet other tennis players at my level than I had hoped. Shortly after I put in my magic box a note with that wish – and released it without attachment – I was playing tennis with fun ladies two to three times a week.

What the above three visualization tools have in common is that they are fun, and they involve collecting artifacts of what you want as if you already have your desires met. Give one of these tools a try, or come up with something that resonates with you.

Again, the precise tool itself is inconsequential, as long as it engages your imagination, thoughts and feelings positively – to train your subconscious mind to believe in the experience of having something, and to broadcast the right signals to call in the desired experience with matching frequencies.

What If I Don't Really Know What I Want?

Some of you may be thinking that all these visualization tools sound good in principle, but they are not useful to you. This is because you do not yet have a clear idea of what you want.

If that describes you, you are in good company. Do not despair, as there are options for you. Years ago, when I was still searching for a satisfying career, I had vague ideas of what I wanted, which surrounded being in a service profession of some sort. The vague ideas of what I wanted in my professional life did not point me clearly to any specific career path.

More importantly, I was a lot more aware of my dissatisfaction with what I was doing to make a living than what would truly excite me. In my search, I came across a fantastic book by Julie Jansen, *I Don't Know What I Want, But I Know It Is Not This*. The title itself grabbed me, because it perfectly described how I felt then.

Through completing a series of exercises in the book, I was able to get clear on what it was that I disliked about my previous jobs and what I would like to have instead. It was all about reviewing where I had been, what I had done, and how these elements lined up with my values and preferences.

In the process, I realized that the career path itself – market research and business consulting – still resonated with me. I discovered that I was still drawn to some elements of the profession, and it did not feel like it was time to walk away from that career just yet. The parts that frustrated me had to do with the companies for which I worked, not the career path itself.

Effectively, I got clarity for what I wanted by starting with analyzing my dissatisfaction. What I needed to do was to find the right employer to continue the same line of work.

With a similar idea, Abraham-Hicks introduced the concept of "pivoting." Whenever we experience something we do not want, the opposite of that is often exactly what we desire. Life presents us with contrasting experiences to what we desire to help us get clear on the latter. Of course, we do not have to experience pain or hardship to know what we want. However, if we do find ourselves in less than desirable circumstances, these are our opportunities to get clear on why we are in agony.

When we are clear about the undesirables, we can then pivot from each of these points onto the thoughts of the opposite. For instance, if you feel overworked and underpaid, use these conditions as points from which to pivot to the opposite, i.e., great work-life balance and being rewarded handsomely for your contributions. Now, don't these sound like things you would want?

Once you have pivoted to the desirable conditions, you can then contemplate further on those conditions. What does it look like to you to have great work-life balance? Does it mean you get to play golf at least once a week, take more day trips on weekends, or have all your evenings and weekends free to do fun things? What does being paid well mean? Can you visualize seeing a larger direct deposit into your bank account with your desired pay? Does it mean you can join that great health club you felt you could not afford?

Ask yourself questions like, *"What does it look like?" "How would it feel when I achieve that?"* This is how you progressively get clarity on what you want.

O *Contemplation Exercise*

- Think of an area in your life in which you would like improvement, e.g., work, relationships, health, etc.

- In your journal or workbook, draw a line down the middle to create two columns. In the first column, list all the conditions with which you are unhappy.

- In the second column, flip each of the conditions in the first column into the opposite, e.g., no time to have fun → ample time to have fun; long, stressful commute → short, easy drive to and from work; no interesting dating prospects → meeting available interesting men/women, etc.

- Once you have your list of pivoted conditions, write more details around what each would look and feel like. For instance, what would you do with the ample time for fun? What fun things would you do? Where may your commute take you? Can you visualize your driving route? What qualities would make for an interesting dating prospect?

Once you have done some contemplation on your pivoted conditions, these become features of your dream situation on which you can practice visualization, using any of the tools we discussed above.

Regardless of the tool you choose, just remember that you want to visualize what you can genuinely believe is true.

Hot Penning

You did some hot penning in the *Release* chapter to uncover your fears and worries about living your dreams, remember that? You can use the very same technique here to help you reveal perhaps some latent discontent about any area of your life you may have suppressed. From there, you can pivot to the conditions on which you can have some visualization fun.

○ *Contemplation Exercise*

Think of an area in your life you would like improvement. Set a timer for 10 minutes, and write whatever comes to mind in response to the following question:

- How do I feel about this area of my life?

Without judgment or censoring, keep writing whatever comes to mind, taking note of any accompanying feelings. Don't stop writing. Make a list if that resonates with you more. Don't worry about grammar, incomplete sentences, spelling, etc., as no one will be reading this. Keep writing from a stream of consciousness until the timer goes off.

Once you are done with this stream-of-consciousness writing, review what you will have written, and make a list of things you want to change. Then, repeat the pivoting exercise above, and use any visualization tool of your choice to start seeing – and feeling – your dream come true!

I hope you see that you can truly have fun envisioning life as if your dreams have already manifested. In the first half of this chapter, we looked at meditations to help us ask the wisest and most creative part of ourselves to reveal our inner dream to us. In the second half, we looked at a series of visualization tools and ways to help us get clear about what we want. If you know what you want, visualization is very powerful. Even if you are clear about your desires, I still highly encourage you to include the visioning and chakra meditations from the first half of the chapter to help you envision your dreams.

By engaging your receptive feminine energy in your envisioning practice, you may receive guidance on inspired action to take, which your rational mind may otherwise miss. We will talk more about taking guided action in the next chapter. Meanwhile, Happy Envisioning!

Summary Points for Envision

❖ We all have an inner dream to be awakened. We can engage our inner creativity to compose the life of our dreams.

❖ Use one or both of the envisioning – visioning and chakra – meditations to receive guidance from your inner creativity. Allow the conditions of your dream to be revealed to you. They may include guidance on actions to take that your rational mind may otherwise miss. Repeat these meditations periodically to check in for new insights.

❖ The visioning meditation will show you the highest vision for your life and your dream, as well as what you need to embrace or become, what you need to release, and anything else you need to know about this vision.

❖ The chakra meditation is designed to seek insights from seven different energy centers in your body associated with different life issues and different levels of needs and desires.

❖ When you have a clear idea of what you want, visualization tools are great for feeling your way into the manifestation of your dreams. For a visualization to work, your subconscious must believe that the imagined experience is real. Therefore, it is important that you choose a scenario that is believable, even if it is a stretch in some way, and that you detach from the outcome. Do not obsess about it, lest you activate the feelings of not having it.

❖ Aside from visualization in your mind's eye, you can create a vision board, scrapbook or magic box – or do something else that resonates with you. Whatever you choose to use, have fun with it!

❖ If you do not know what you want, create a list of conditions you do not want. Do some hot penning, if it would help, and pivot from each undesirable point to the opposite condition. Then, visualize on the pivoted desired conditions.

CHAPTER 4

Act

*"Inaction breeds doubt and fear.
Action breeds confidence and courage.
If you want to conquer fear,
don't sit at home and think about it.
Go out and get busy."*
— Dale Carnegie

Let's take a moment and ponder the above advice from an influential voice in personal development, shall we? You just spent some time in the last chapter letting your inner dream unfold, getting clarity on your desires in at least one area of your life.

How long can that juiciness last if you don't start doing something toward realizing the dream? How long can you sit idly before the excitement fizzles out, before fears and doubts take over? Do you really want to, once again, let the demands of your daily life drown out that inner dream? Can you really feed your dream and make it real without springing into action, even if it is one baby step at a time?

As important as it is to go out and get busy, please allow me to stress that not all action is conducive to making dreams come true. Busy action reacting to life will not do. Instead, we need purposeful and thoughtful action spawned by our inner wisdom and creativity, the same source that unveiled the dream to us in the first place.

Modern life has adopted such an unfortunate manic pace that there is no time to breathe and just be. It seems that something is wrong unless we are in constant motion. To exacerbate matters, with the prevalence of more and different types of electronic media and communication gadgets, we are wired and connected all the time. We are constantly inundated with information, and there is an unspoken expectation of near-instantaneous response to any communication.

Meanwhile, time has not expanded to accommodate the growing expectations of doing more that has been enabled by technological advances. Living with all this busyness, when do we have time to think and reflect, let alone act with purpose and thoughtfulness?

Unless we become mindful of why we act, we continue to perpetuate the cycle of reacting to life instead of creating it. Our dreams do not thrive when we operate in a reactive mode filled with busy action. They require us to pay attention and follow the inspiration and guidance from our inner wisdom and creativity.

In this chapter, we will take a closer look at what it means to take guided, inspired action on our dreams. This includes first getting clear on why we want to take action – or not. Once we are ready to take guided action, we need to be able to discern the difference between guidance from our inner wisdom vs. our ego. We will then talk about how to cultivate a practice of tuning into guidance.

This chapter will close with walking you through how to develop a guided action plan for your dream that is SMART – Specific, Measurable, Actionable, Realistic and Time-trackable.

Are you ready to take SMART action on your dream?

Why Do You Want to Act (or Not)?

So far in this book, we have talked quite a bit about fear keeping us trapped where we are, because the status quo is familiar, even if it does not make us happy. Feeding on the dark side of passive feminine energy, our ego tells us it is best to stay put, as it is unsafe to go anywhere else.

We have not talked as much about fear propelling us to run because we are afraid to stand still. Running away from the status quo constitutes action out of desperation, not inspiration. In this scenario, that part of us which is our ego is filled up with unhealthy, aggressive masculine energy. It urges us to manage our fear by doing something about the perceived threatening situation. We need to run away to restore our feelings of being in control.

As you read previously in this book, I went through much of my life over-compensating for my feelings of inferiority and lack of self-worth. As a by-product of this drive to succeed, I equated standing still to failure. In fact, my mantra could easily have been, *"If I'm not moving forward, I might as well be dead!"* This survivor-fighter instinct enabled me to overcome and achieve a lot. But, let me tell you, acting primarily out of fear is an unnecessarily hard way to live.

We always have a choice in whether to act or not act. If the inclination is to act, realize that there is a fine line between taking action for the sake of not standing still and following an inspiration toward something.

The need to discern these choices is precisely the sage advice offered by Gregg Levoy in *Callings: Finding and Following An Authentic Life* (pg. 254):

> "Before taking a leap, establish whether a particular status quo in your life is a monument to the fear of change, and whether the risk to which you are attracted is a function of sheer restlessness and ennui. Nothing is inherently wrong with either status quo or restlessness, but if you are taking chances and making changes just for the sake of not standing still, your actions may be more about running away from some-

thing than moving toward something. Motion is not necessarily progress any more than noise is necessarily music."

In all likelihood, if you have a dream, it lures you to it. The power of the pull depends on the size of your dream and how much busy life static it has to cut through to get your attention. This is especially true if your life circumstances are less than ideal, and a part of you only wants to run away from them. If you are not hurting though, would you still want to change anything about your life? Your answer to this question would indicate whether you are running out of fear or being inspired to go toward a dream.

Also, either of the two meditations from the *Envision* chapter – visioning and chakra – would give you good insights on whether your desire to act is aligned with your inner dream or motivated by something else.

As Levoy points out, there is nothing inherently wrong with standing still or running away. If you feel compelled to do either, honor that. After all, we are exactly where we need to be at any given point in time. We have the free will to change or not change. I urge you to choose deliberately and consciously, instead of acting – or not – reflexively out of fear or a habit of sticking with what is familiar. Know why you are staying put or from what you are trying to flee, lest you wonder why you seem to be stuck or be in perpetual motion without becoming happier.

And, if your pain is so great that you need to escape first to address your survival needs, please honor that, too. Just realize that leaving the status quo is only the intermediate step for manifesting your dream; further action down the road is necessary.

My two-stage transition into doing REACH work is a case in point. I promised myself that being a self-employed business consultant was only meant to be an intermediate step. My REACH dream remained steadfast in my consciousness. I continued to listen for guidance, to ready myself mentally, psychologically and spiritually to step fully into my dream – to help you REACH yours – when I was finally ready.

○ *Contemplation Exercise*

- Take a moment to reflect on what you want to change in your life. Is it a dream or a desire pulling you toward it, or is it about a situation you no longer want in your life?

- Are you ready to take action on this change? Why or why not? Be honest with yourself. No one is looking or judging you. Honor your response either way.

Before you leap into action, be mindful of why you want to do that, whether you are running away from your life or toward your dream. If your dream is big, be prepared to break it down into chunks that honor what you are ready to do in the short vs. the long term. We will talk more about breaking down your dream later in this chapter.

If you deliberately and consciously choose not to take any action, know your reasons and honor them. Cut yourself some slack, and do not chastise yourself for being too chicken to do anything about the status quo.

Allow me to say this much, however: If you do feel even the slightest inkling of a dream, a higher-level desire above mere survival, visit with it periodically. Allow the seed of your dream to germinate and bud. In time, this plant of desire will oxygenate your consciousness. In turn, this positive life force energy will propel you forward, beckoning you to allow it to carry you to your dream.

True Inner Guidance vs. Ego-Based Directives

Now that you have made a conscious decision to act on your dream, the next order of business is to follow guidance from your inner wisdom and creativity.

At this point, you may be wondering: How do I know whether it is truly guidance from my soul and not directives from that part of me which is my ego? After all, both sources come from within.

Good question. Let's talk about some defining characteristics of true guidance.

You vs. *I*

The highest and wisest part of us channels cosmic wisdom for our expansion and growth. It is not identified with itself, and therefore addresses us in the second person. If you get inner guidance, say, to leave your job, the message to you may be: *Leave your job now.*

By contrast, in its vested interests in keeping us safe, the part of us which is our ego is self-identified. Therefore, its directives tend to come in the first person. The same job advice may sound more like: *I gotta leave this job because it is killing me.*

The first message addresses you in the second person, while your ego's message consists of an "I" statement. So, pay attention to how you are addressed in the messages you receive.

Motivated by Love vs. Fear

Ego-based directives are typically motivated by fear to control a situation or others' behavior that threatens our feelings of safety. When we feel that people have to act a certain way, or an event has to happen in a very specific timeframe, in a specific manner, these are telltale signs of our ego's signature advice.

Similarly, when we find ourselves seeking *external* validation and acceptance, our ego is likely in the driver seat as well. We worry about how others may react to our actions or inaction – *they may not like me; they may think that I'm not a team-player*, etc. When we feel the need to do something for someone in order to ingratiate them or to fish for compliments, there is a good chance our ego is pulling our strings.

By contrast, guidance from our inner voice is motivated by love. The highest and wisest part of ourselves always seeks growth and expansion, and it knows that love is the ultimate source energy that powers everything and everyone. Therefore, even if the guidance we get from our inner wisdom often stretches our comfort, it is always motivated by love.

When we feel an inner call to grow, to invoke the power within to compose any life we wish to create, this expansive nudge is from our inner wisdom. Unlike ego-based directives, such inner guidance does not lead us to seek external approval. Everything we need to make our dreams a reality comes from *within* ourselves. We do not need others' approval, just our own permission and willingness.

To give you an example, you may recall from the Prologue that I was guided to harvest the love in my heart. This message came when I meditated for my soul's highest vision for me in 2011.

Had I asked my ego for advice instead, the message would likely have been very different. After all, our ego's specialty is to take control always; our survival is too important to be left up to chance.

However, my soul knows there is nothing in my external life for me to orchestrate. What is mine to do is to continue to grow in love, be the woman I want to be, and follow inner guidance on action that is mine to take. In short, my to-do is to continue to awaken inner grace. That is the love I was guided to harvest within my own heart.

Direct and Succinct

Our inner wisdom gets right to the point. It does not qualify a message, unless we ask for further information. So, true inner guidance is direct and succinct. For instance, when I asked about my next steps in my career, the message I got was: *Leave now. Trust that something better will come to you.*

There was no back story about why I should leave. It just spelled out in crystal clear terms what action I needed to take. I could – and I did – choose to continue to dialogue with my inner wisdom about the time frame and ramifications. It answered each of my questions succinctly without offering any further explanation.

By contrast, when our ego speaks, usually there is an unsolicited back story to go with its messages – especially a grievance story of some sort. The motivation behind wanting us to act is fear-based, and the goal is to control the situation to avoid being controlled by it.

Let me give you an example to which you may be able to relate. I have a loved one who unknowingly tests others' love for her constantly. The running test is: *If they love me, they would do this for me. If they don't do it, they don't love me.* The score resets after each test, so this do-you-love-me test is a bottomless pit.

I have learned not to step into it. After all, coddling this unhealthy behavior ultimately does not fill the void within her that only she can fill. Meanwhile, I would be dishonoring my own integrity and boundaries.

One day, after not having seen or talked with her for a while, I called her to check in. When she did not pick up, I left a voicemail and went back to my day in-progress – writing this book.

Before long, I became aware of the escalating inner dialogue: *Why didn't she pick up the phone? I know she's there. I bet she's mad at me. I can't believe this. This is getting so old. But, maybe I should call her again.*

Otherwise, it will only get worse. I really don't want to have to deal with the guilt trips again. I don't want to be told again that I don't care. It's so not true, and I'm sick of it! It's never enough. I should just call her again and nip this in the bud.

On and on the back story rolled. As the story built, feelings of guilt and worry mounted also. Before I knew it, I was just about convinced that I would have a crisis in my hands if I did not pick up the phone to call her again. I suspect you can relate to this story.

Luckily, I did know enough to recognize that it was my ego talking, fearful of incurring the wrath of the other person. When I realized who was talking, I was able to tell myself that I already did my part lovingly by initiating contact and letting her know that I was thinking of her. This person's response was not mine to control. If she would like to talk, she could call me back. There was no reason to feel guilty or apprehensive. I did not need to manage this situation any further. The sky would not fall if she chose not to call back for any reason.

In case you are curious, about five minutes after I settled this with my ego, the phone rang. Guess who it was?

Aside from having a back story, an ego-based directive also tends to come with strong attachments to a very specific outcome. That is, we believe we cannot be happy unless we land a particular job or possess the love of a certain person.

When I was coaching a young friend recently on his job transition, I urged him not to get emotionally attached to getting any specific job for which he might be interviewing. Instead, it would be in his best interests to focus his energy and envisioning on the conditions he would like to have in his new job – the kinds of colleagues and clients he would like to have, the nature of the work he wants to do, how far he would like to commute, etc. It is important for him not to get attached to any specific opportunity.

When he meditated, the guidance he got was not about working for any particular employer. Instead, it was about the broader conditions which would bring him more satisfaction all around and allow him to grow professionally.

In sum, inner wisdom from our soul does not direct us to control the external circumstances of our lives – including the people in them – or to get hung up on the specifics. Therefore, its messages to us are always direct and to the point. When we feel a call to act, and it comes with a back story and strong emotional attachments to a specific outcome, there is a good chance it is our take-no-chances ego talking.

Recurring Nudging

You may recall from the *Release* chapter that, when our soul knows we are ready to grow, it will continue to nudge us to change something in our lives. The same message gets louder and louder in time, until we do something about the call.

I already shared with you some examples before, including my repeated call to leave my last employer in November 2009. I kept hearing a soundless voice repeating "November" to me. The repetitive dream I had about my failing marriage is another case in point; my inner wisdom jolted me on a nightly basis for months to make a much needed life change.

That part of us which is our ego is quite tenacious and persistent as well. However, what our ego repeats tends to be derivatives of the same grievance story, triggered by the cumulative pain from the unchanged situation. If the undesirable situation has persisted for some time, there is often reprimand in the back story as well.

In other words, whereas the recurring message from our inner wisdom remains direct and succinct, our ego's lines revolve around the back story and the pain. The story may go something like this: *Here we go again. How many times does this have to happen before I get my act together and leave? What am I, a frigging doormat?!? Do I have no self-respect left? How much more am I willing to take? I gotta get outta here!*

When you feel recurring nudging to do something, pay attention to what is being repeated. Is it the same direct and succinct call to action, regardless of how many times it has been issued? Or is it the cumulative pain – and escalating shame – from enduring the same undesirable situation?

○ *Contemplation Exercise*

Think of a recent time when you felt an inner nudge to do something, whether it is big or small.

- How did it address you – "You" or "I"?
- Did it nudge you to have the courage to allow yourself to do something? Or did it nudge you to seek validation from someone else or to take pre-emptive action?
- Was the message direct and succinct, or did it come with a back story and attachment to a specific outcome – along with associated emotions?
- Was this a message you have received before? If so, what was repeated?

What did your answers tell you about your recent nudging? Was it from your inner wisdom or ego? If you are unsure, review the defining characteristics of guidance from your soul vs. your ego. Next time you receive a message or feel a nudge to do something, you can repeat this exercise to get clarity. In time, you will quickly recognize which part of you is talking.

Cultivating Receptivity to Inner Guidance

Most of us in the modern world are a lot more comfortable running our masculine (Yang) energy than our feminine (Yin) energy. These include us women, who have spent much of our lives developing our intellectual/analytical capabilities and building careers in the rational corporate world.

Regardless of our sex, we all need our take-charge, get-things-done masculine energy to keep us moving forward. Otherwise, we will not accomplish anything. However, relying solely on our Yang energy is lop-sided, engaging only half of ourselves; it leaves the other half of our personal power unused. What a shame!

Our intuitive feminine energy is invaluable when it comes to realizing our dreams. It gets us into a state of receptivity, allowing us to tune into our inner guidance and cosmic wisdom. When we allow our Yin and Yang energies to operate together – that's why we have both! – they complement each other and make a complete and effective manifestation team.

To trade our lop-sided overuse of masculine energy for a more balanced way of living, we need practice running our Yin energy. And the best form of practice is meditation.

Meditation gets us into the silence between thoughts. We need silence from mind chatter and ego-based directives to allow our inner voice to come forward. It creates a receptive space in our consciousness and a direct pathway to cosmic wisdom and guidance from our soul. In this space, we are free to see, hear, feel, and/or know what wants our attention.

We do not have to meditate for hours every day to create this silent space, but regular practice is crucial. As meditation becomes a habit in your life, you will start to feel more tuned into the source energy of the universe. Noticing inner guidance and synchronicities will come more naturally to you.

If you already have a meditation practice, please keep it up. If you have thought about or dabbled in one, I strongly encourage you to try (again). Find a method or style that suits you, and stick with it.

If you are new to meditation, begin with just 5 minutes a day. Set a timer for that and relax. Close your eyes, and take a couple of slow deep breaths. Feel each breath expanding not just your lungs but your belly. As you breathe in, imagine yourself breathing in the energy of love from the universe, and feel that love gradually filling up your body. As you exhale, feel the tension, stress and worries your body has been holding slowly being melted away and released. Repeat the above until the timer goes off.

A similar technique to the above is a body scan. As you breathe, notice sensations in different parts of your body, from the bottom of your feet to the top of your head. It does not matter where you start, but you want to move slowly through each section, i.e., feet, ankles, calves, knees, thighs and so on. As you take a breath in, notice what you feel in a particular section. With each breath out, release any tension in that part of your body. A tremendous amount of insight comes through our body. The more we tune into our physical sensations, the more we tap into the wisdom channeled through our body.

If you are a visual person, an easy way to meditate is to focus on pleasant imagery. Picture yourself somewhere that is serene, relaxing and safe. For instance, you may recall in previous chapters that I directed you to a safe place in your mind's eye when guiding you through meditations. As you breathe in and out, just notice what is in that picture. Is it out in nature? What kinds of trees do you see? What is the quality of the lighting? Let the imagery hold you as you relax into this silent, safe space.

If you are verbal, try focusing on mantras or simple words. For instance, as you take a breath in, you can say to yourself with your inner voice, "*I welcome love.*" As you breathe out, say, "*I release all resistance.*" You can also focus on a single word, such as "*Love,*" "*Peace,*" "*Joy,*" "*Grace,*" "*Ohm.*" Pick any word that is affirming and personally meaningful to you.

When distractions come up during meditation, just notice them without judgment, and return your focus to your breath, imagery, word, etc. When mind chatter shows up, or you start planning your day or ruminating over something going on in your life, just notice that, and say to yourself, "*Later.*" Don't get upset or frustrated with yourself that you cannot even spend 5 minutes meditating. The human mind is very active. Its job is to produce thoughts. Just notice that your mind has wandered, and say to yourself, "*Later.*"

O *Meditation Practice*

- Set a timer for 5 minutes, and meditate using one of the above techniques.

- Starting tomorrow, pick a set time to do another 5-minute meditation, repeating the same technique or trying a different one. Make it a habit of doing this every day at the same time, ideally first thing in the morning.

- When you are ready, increase your meditation time to 10 minutes, then 15 minutes, and so on. You do not need to meditate for hours. But, it needs to be regular.

- Feel free to substitute in the visioning or chakra meditation from the last chapter – or any other meditation of your choice.

It is beyond the scope or purpose of this book to engage in an exhaustive discussion of the benefits of meditation. Suffice it to say that a regular meditation practice will likely bring you more calmness and grounding in your daily life. And, of course, you will develop your ability to tune into your inner guidance for actions to take to realize your dream. You have learned meditations for this specific purpose in the last chapter.

There are other ways guidance comes to us, including through our intuition, dreams when we are asleep, and all kinds of synchronicities. You can read more about these in the *Epilogue* of this book. As you get more in tune with your feminine side through meditation, your awareness of these other forms of insights will likely be heightened as well.

In short, there are many reasons to maintain a regular meditation practice. Even 5 minutes a day on a sustained basis will do wonders for you – and your dream. If you do not yet have a meditation practice, develop one.

Take SMART Action

We have covered how to recognize guidance and how to access it through meditation. Are you ready to roll up your sleeves to take action on your dream? Or does the enormity of your dream seem overwhelming or intimidating at this point, and you do not have a good idea of where to start?

If you are in the second category, know that your reaction is normal. Therefore, feel no shame; you are in good company. Dreams are mesmerizing because of their magnetic pull. However, they are also rarely close to the reality of where we are at the present time. That is why so many of us feel the conflict of wanting something of which we are also afraid. After all, going after our dreams often requires us to stretch our comfort – do something we have never attempted before, be someone we never believed we could be previously.

Aside from challenging our comfort level, if our dream is big, it can feel tantamount to having to move a mountain to make it happen. In other words, it is one tall order of a project that would intimidate anyone.

But, what if we break this enormous project down into smaller, manageable ones that involve moving a bunch of rocks at a time? When we complete each of these smaller tasks in time, they eventually add up to moving the mountain. These smaller tasks do not seem so insurmountable, do they?

In short, have manageable goals, focus on taking action on one goal at a time, and we are less likely to be scared off. In time, these goals will add up to the realization of our dream. In this section, I will walk you through precisely how to do just that.

For many of you, you will be happy to know that you are about to venture back into familiar territory. You will be engaging your in-control, take-care-of-business masculine energy, specifically the healthy side.

For the rest of you, this will exercise the unfamiliar Yang part of you. Don't worry, as I will walk you through planning actions step by step. Promise you will give this seemingly foreign way of doing things a chance, though. Keep your end reward in sight: Your dream come true!

To take action on your dream, let me introduce you to an effective action planning and tracking tool. It is based on a widely used, proven project management technique called SMART. You literally get to be SMART with your dream – how about that?!

SMART is a mnemonic for Specific, Measurable, Actionable, Realistic and Time-trackable. Using SMART, you can define goals for actions to take toward fulfilling your dream.

Let's look at the SMART components in turn.

Specific

First, you want to break down your dream into small, discrete goals that can be acted upon one by one over time. Include any insights you got from your meditations or other guidance about your dream. Ultimately, when you achieve all these specific goals, your dream will be a reality. The idea here is to break down something big into manageable chunks. Keep getting more specific, until the goal or action step itself cannot be reduced any further.

For instance, if your dream is to have a more satisfying career, what are specific, manageable chunks of this dream? Perhaps, one specific part is to define clearly what your dream career looks like. If you have not already done so, use any of the envisioning tools from the last chapter.

Following that, you may need to assess which of your skills and experiences are transferrable to your dream career, and where there may be gaps. In the case of gaps, you may need to explore how best to fill them. Perhaps, you will need to take some classes or get yourself transferred to another department in your company where you can gain some relevant experience.

For now, let's follow the thread of taking classes to define more specific goals. What does taking classes entail? Does it mean first getting course catalogs from area colleges offering continuing education? What about doing some research online? Would you need to talk to people who are already in your dream career to get ideas about continuing education? What else would you do to find out about classes that teach you the skills you need for your next career?

Each of the ways to get clear on what you need becomes a specific goal. In sum, the beginning list of your specific goals may look like this:

1. Define what my dream career looks like by doing the hot penning and pivoting exercises in the *Envision* chapter.

2. List all of my skills and experiences to date. Evaluate which ones are transferrable to my dream career, and what gaps I may need to fill.
3. Request catalogs from the three colleges in my area.
4. Do research online for where else I can take classes.
5. Schedule an interview with Sue in Marketing to ask her about classes that may help me learn relevant skills.

Do you see how this works? Each of the above five goals is a discrete activity. Instead of getting overwhelmed by the entire dream of switching careers, you can focus on one activity at a time. The more specific you get with your goals, the more likely you will complete them. In the end, your entire plan will lead you to your dream – provided you follow through with action, of course.

Measurable

Aside from getting specific about your goals, you would want to set ones that are measurable as well. A great way to set measurable goals is to make sure you can check them off when they are done.

Looking at the short list above, each of these steps can be checked off. When a goal is not something you can check off easily, chances are it is not measurable, and may be not specific enough.

As another example, if you would like to lose weight, and you set your goal as "Make exercise a priority." Well, can you check that off? How do you know whether exercise has become a priority or not?

Alternatively, let's say your goal is something like, "Go for a 20-minute walk around my neighborhood every evening after dinner." That is definitely more specific and something you can check off. You either have or have not gone for a walk a particular day. And, you can count whether it did in fact last 20 minutes.

Actionable

Another important ingredient for a good action plan is that your goals must lead you to action. Great but abstract ideas do not make for a good action plan.

Let's say you want to meditate regularly to develop your connection to your inner guidance. What would you set as your *actionable* goal for "meditating regularly"? Perhaps, it is something like, "Starting tomorrow and for one full week, I will meditate for 5 minutes first thing every morning before I do anything else." A goal like this is specific, something you can check off at the end of one week, and it clearly spells out what action you will take.

Realistic

When what we set out to do is so big that it stretches us too much too fast, we risk feeling resistance to it, getting discouraged, and giving up. Set your goals big enough to move you out of the status quo gradually, but not so big that it feels too scary a leap.

I cannot prescribe for you what that looks like precisely, because only you know how far you are ready to stretch yourself. Much like what we talked about with making your visualization believable, you want your goals to be realistically what you can act on.

If you are a night owl, setting a goal to do an exercise boot camp at 5:30am every morning is simply unrealistic – and you will feel crummy if you do not accomplish your goal. Why set yourself up to fail? Instead, you will be more likely to stick with something later in the day.

Time-trackable

Last, but not least, try to bind your goals within a timeframe. Goals with clear start and end dates have a much higher chance of being achieved. You are less likely to forget about a goal if there is a start and an end date. Some examples are, "Starting tomorrow, I will…"; "By April 1, I will have…"

When you find it challenging to set an end date for your goal, it is usually a sign that one or more of the above action planning elements is/are missing.

For instance, your goal may not be specific enough. You may have the overall good intention of exercising more, so an end date seems irrelevant. However, if you think about it, that overall intention will probably look different over time. You can always set a goal for going to a certain exercise class in the next 3 months. After that time, you will re-evaluate whether you like it and whether it is effective. Then, you can decide whether to continue or do something else.

While the intention of exercising more may not have an end date, the specifics of how you do it can always be bound by a timeframe.

Another reason why you may have difficulty binding a goal within a timeframe is when the goal is outside of your control. You cannot easily set a deadline for someone else's behavior, nor can you dictate how soon the universe aligns events to fulfill your goal. Unless you are already a manifestation master, and you are sure you have absolutely no hidden barriers left in your creative field, setting a deadline by which someone else or the universe needs to respond will likely lead to disappointment. Again, why set yourself up to be disappointed?

Instead, set goals on the parts of your dream over which you have complete control. Usually, those have to do with preparing yourself.

Let's say that your dream is to be (re-)married by a certain time in your life. Reframe that into an intention around which you can develop specific goals on which you can take conscious action. Your reframed intention may be something like, "In the next 6 months, I intend to prepare myself to be the woman/man for whom I want to be loved by my spouse." From that intention, you can set specific goals around releasing any and all lingering self-limiting beliefs, getting clear about what being a happily married person feels like, and envisioning that, and so on.

In short, your plan is about taking steps to become the wife/husband for whom you want to be loved – to become magnetic to your dream. Even though nothing in your plan ostensibly states you will be married by a certain time, by readying yourself, the external circumstances of your life must align themselves to match the evolved you. We talked about that before; it is by universal law that this must happen.

When doing action planning, the timeframe itself needs to be as realistic as the goals you set. If your goals are too ambitious time-wise, you run the risk of not being able to achieve them. Once you miss a few goals, instead of REACHing your dream, it suddenly feels very much out of reach – pun intended!

So, let me repeat: Don't set yourself up to fail. Give yourself time.

Creating Your SMART Plan

Now that you have been introduced to the components of a SMART plan, you are ready to create your own. Before we dive in, let me offer a few observations about maximizing your success with your SMART plan.

First of all, be sure to incorporate what is revealed to you in your envisioning meditations or other forms of intuitive guidance, i.e., insights that meet the true guidance criteria but which you may not be able to explain logically. (See *Epilogue* for further details.) Be careful not to set goals solely around your conscious desires. As you have probably found, your inner wisdom and creativity may have other ideas for you that elude your rational mind. Follow that guidance, and you are more likely to be taking critical steps toward realizing your dream.

Secondly, know thyself when creating your action plan. Forgive me for being blunt, but please be honest about any self-sabotaging tendencies you may have. If you tend to be overly ambitious and impatient, challenge yourself to be realistic about how many goals you can really accomplish in a short amount of time.

Take into consideration what else you have going on in your life, and how much time and space you can honestly devote to your SMART goals. You may feel that things could not happen fast enough for you – trust me, I can relate! However, it truly is better for things to come more slowly than not at all.

Conversely, if you tend to view plans as suggestive guidelines instead of a firm commitment to act, challenge yourself to stay true to acting on your goals. Consider building in some accountability measures in your action plan.

For instance, ask someone who knows you well and whom you respect to work through setting realistic and actionable goals with you. Give them the permission to hold you accountable for your plan. They do not have to be punitive, but allow them to nag you about following through. You may not like it, but it is for your ultimate good.

Remember, no matter how palpable your dream feels, it does not become a reality if you do not take action. Really commit to doing this for your own good.

By nature, I am a chart-the-course planner. Breaking big goals down into realistic, time-bounded chunks is just about second nature to me. Therefore, years before I heard of SMART project management, I was already applying the same principles in my life. That was how I managed to finish my doctoral dissertation (essentially a book) in half the time I would otherwise have – while under great duress.

The time pressure was for a great cause: A tenure-track assistant professorship was waiting for me at Cornell University. For that, I had to finish my doctoral studies a semester ahead of schedule.

As for the duress, my seven-year marriage (nine-year relationship) came to an end. At age 27, my identity was wrapped up around being someone's wife. As a result, my world as I knew it was crumbling at a disheartening rate – even as a new life and a new identity were being written simultaneously.

Under those high-stress circumstances, I could not allow myself to think of the entire task at hand, lest I became paralyzed by its enormity. I had only two months to write up a 180-page technical dissertation on my original research – which I had to complete in record time as well. I knew I had to break down the writing into manageable chunks for each week in those two months. And, I would only focus on one week at a time, just as I would survive my mind-numbing, heart-breaking divorce one day at a time.

That was how I managed to get my Ph.D. in time to begin my Cornell appointment. At the time, the perfectionist in me thought my dissertation was mediocre. I was convinced that I would have done a better job if I had more time. Instead, I had to be ok with having done the best I could with the time I had. To my surprise, it ended up winning a dissertation award given by a major professional association in my field!

My intention for telling you this story, especially the last part, is not to brag. Instead, the point I want to make is this: SMART action planning really works! It can truly help you realize your dream.

This is regardless of how intimidating your dream may seem in its totality. It also does not matter how much duress you may be under while trying to make your dream a reality. If you really want it, all you have to do is break it down into bite-size chunks that you can realistically manage, given your situation. Then, focus on one SMART goal at a time, one day at a time. These goals will eventually add up to the manifestation of your dream!

With all of the above said, are you ready to create your very own SMART plan for your dream?

- First, in your journal or workbook, list 3 SMART goals – give or take – you would like to set for the next month. Be sure to include any steps revealed to you in your envisioning meditations or from other sources of intuitive guidance.

- Following the SMART Plan template below, create a similar grid on a large piece of paper or poster board.

- In the first column under "Action", you will enter each of the goals you wrote down in your journal/workbook. Remember to be as specific as you can. Each goal should take up one row in the grid.

- Enter the "Start Date" you plan to begin each goal and the "Due Date" you plan to finish it.

My Smart Action Plan

Action	Start Date	Due Date	What may keep me from taking action?	How can I address this obstacle?	How will I celebrate achieving this goal?

To get this book written, I have been following a SMART plan myself. I first set my intention on when I wanted the book to be completed. Then, I broke that overall intention down into specific goals when each individual chapter would be completed. I adjusted the plan slightly, after asking myself to be honest about whether it was realistic – once an over-achiever, always an over-achiever!

I have been able to follow this plan and check chapters off as they were written. While the order in which I have been writing the chapters kept changing – I have been following where my inspiration takes me – I have been able to stay within the overall timeframe set. It gives me a great sense of accomplishment each time I get to check off another finished chapter.

Preparing for Show Stoppers

Despite the best of intentions, it seems that the best laid plans can be derailed by distractions. The same goes for your SMART plan. Of course, there are distractions we cannot anticipate, such as an unexpected family emergency needing our attention.

However, if we are really honest with ourselves, in all likelihood, most distractions do not come out of the left field. Yes, we are talking about our old friend from the *Release* chapter again: *legitimate* excuses. Let's face it, when something truly is important to us, we *always* have the time and energy for it, don't we? Conversely, when we procrastinate on something about which we simply are not that excited, what do we say? *"I'm sorry, but I was too busy to get to it,"* right?

The same excuse-producing apparatus is likely to affect your SMART plan, too. After all, acting on our dream likely stretches our comfort. That part of us which is our ego would rather we stay in our comfort zone and not do anything to threaten the safety of the status quo. It stands armed and ready to manufacture all kinds of *legitimate* reasons – a.k.a. excuses – for why we should not take action.

You may have experienced this. When you know there is something important for you to do, but it stretches your comfort, everything else all of a sudden becomes more important. Cleaning your bathroom when you normally hate this chore, catching up on the past seasons of a TV show you never watched before, feeling the need to run an errand that has no real urgency – these are just some examples. You get the picture.

If it ever feels like something else has more pull than one of your SMART goals, let that be a signal to you that there is likely some hidden resistance you need to clear. Is your goal too big for where you are now? Do you need to break it down further into more realistic steps? Can you use some moral support to make sure you stay on track? Is the timeframe you set for achieving this goal too aggressive? Are you, once again, being sucked into the undercurrent of seemingly legitimate reasons why you cannot do this?

In *Excuses Begone!*, the late Dr. Wayne Dyer offers an in-depth look at why it is human nature to produce excuses to procrastinate. He says that blame is generally behind our excuses. Think about it. When we claim we are too busy, we are blaming our inaction on the lack of time. When we say we are not smart enough, we are blaming our lack of natural abilities, perhaps even our genetic heritage.

Regardless of the specifics, when we catch ourselves slipping into a blaming mode, we can choose to shift our focus to more constructive thoughts to ward off the tendency to procrastinate. One suggestion he offers is that we ask ourselves this question: *How may I serve?* This thought shifts our energy and focus to that of giving, away from wallowing in the powerlessness of whatever we feel limits us.

For the purposes of your SMART goals, think about how you may serve once your dream is realized. Does your dream involve being of service in some way? If so, every time you find yourself drifting into your ego-orchestrated blame game, imagine how good it would feel to be able to serve when your dream is fulfilled.

Even if your dream does not have an overt service component, just by being a happier, more fulfilled person, you make a better life partner, family member, friend, colleague, community member and fellow citizen of Planet Earth. Doesn't it make you feel better to focus on that instead of the reasons why you cannot act on your SMART goals?

Why am I bringing all this up now, when you are barely starting to define your SMART goals? I want you to anticipate likely excuses and to be prepared to head off these potential show-stoppers.

Knowing yourself and your life – again, be very honest with yourself – what will likely come up to distract you from acting on each of your goals? If demands on your time are big, how can you make sure you protect time for each goal? How about scheduling a standing appointment with yourself that is reserved for your SMART goals?

Treat it just like you would with a client or business partner, as if it is a work assignment that you know you will honor. If lacking discipline is a possible show stopper, how about carrying out that goal with someone who can hold you accountable and make it fun? If you get discouraged easily, how about scheduling a celebration with a friend, so that you have an incentive to finish the goal, the reason to celebrate?

I am asking you all these hard questions now because I want you to succeed. Yes, it is tough love, I know. But, trust me, doing your homework now to prepare for roadblocks will pay dividends when you actually meet them on your path to your dream. You will be grateful you are prepared.

- Back to the SMART plan you started developing, for each goal, please answer the two questions in the heading of the fourth and fifth columns:
  - What may keep me from taking action?
  - How can I address this obstacle?

We will talk about the last column in your SMART Plan in the next chapter – *Celebrate*. Otherwise, you are ready to start acting on your SMART Plan – how exciting!

After you have completed each goal, be sure to check or cross it off, so that it visually shows the progress you are making. As you complete your goals, set new ones for the next month and the month after that – until your dream has been fulfilled. Again, set about 3 goals per month to keep the momentum going. Be sure to include any new inner guidance you may have received.

As you continue SMART planning, depending on your nature, either avoid being too ambitious or commit to following through. Think of your SMART Plan as a living, evolving document to help you set goals and track your actions toward your dreams. Have fun with it!

Summary Points for Act

❖ Make a deliberate and conscious choice on taking action or not. If you choose to take action, recognize whether it is an intermediate step to get away from your current situation or it is to go toward your dream.

❖ True guidance addresses you in the second person, is motivated by love for your growth and expansion, is direct and succinct, and can be the same recurring nudging. Ego-based directives are "I" messages, are motivated by fear to control a situation or others, seek external validation, come with strong attachments to specific outcomes, and tend to repeat a cumulative grievance story.

❖ We tune into our inner wisdom and creativity through meditation. It creates a silent space for engaging our feminine energy to receive guidance on what action to take. We do not have to meditate for hours, but it needs to be regular.

❖ Start creating your SMART action plan by breaking down your dream into specific, measurable, actionable, realistic and time-trackable goals to be acted upon over time. Follow the template provided in this chapter.

❖ Aim for about 3 goals per month, and focus on one month at a time. Check each one off as it is accomplished, and develop new ones for the next month. When all the goals are accomplished, your dream becomes a reality.

❖ Be sure to include insights from your meditations and other intuitive guidance. Do not set goals only based on your conscious desires, lest you miss something your inner wisdom knows that eludes your rational mind.

❖ Be honest with yourself, and be mindful of your self-sabotaging tendencies. If you tend to be overly ambitious, challenge yourself to set realistic goals and due dates. If you tend to be lax about following through, build accountability measures in your action plan.

❖ Knowing yourself and your life, anticipate what may keep you from taking action on your SMART goals. Think about how each potential show stopper can be addressed.

CHAPTER 5

Celebrate

*"The more you praise and celebrate your life,
the more there is in life to celebrate."*
— Oprah Winfrey

Recently, I had the most delightful experience celebrating life with a dear friend of mine. We went to a day-long Abraham-Hicks workshop on *"Getting Into the Vortex."* I have cited Abraham-Hicks throughout this book.

What they call the *"Vortex of Creation"* is really the energy field of our inner wisdom and love, the highest and most creative part of ourselves that is connected to source energy. The vortex is resistance-free and, in it, we fully allow love, abundance, joy and wellbeing of all forms to flow. As such, while we are in the vortex we can manifest anything. Our radio is tuned to the frequencies of experiences that match the desires of our fearless, limitless higher self. When we are outside the vortex, our radio is tuned to the wrong channel for our desires.

Anyway, my friend and I came away from the workshop beaming from the high energy of being in our respective vortex. We really felt our individual connection with source energy and the collective vibrations we shared.

After that vortex workshop, we were both eager for more, wanting to stretch out the great joy of being able to share that day of learning with each other. We wanted to dwell in the engrossing collective energy enveloping us. So, we ended up having a lovely and energizing visit over tea at my house afterwards. It was one of the most enjoyable celebrations of life I remember having in a long time. It was pure bliss! Even as I am writing about this delicious experience, every fiber of my being remembers that day as if it is happening right now. Every cell in my body is soaking up this wonderful celebratory energy all over again.

I choose the above story with which to open this chapter because celebration is often overlooked in our lives. We tend to think of celebrations only for major achievements (e.g., a promotion, winning an award, graduation, etc.) or significant life events (e.g., weddings, births, birthdays, etc.). These are obviously great occasions to break out the bubbly and the party hats, and it is important to continue to celebrate these big moments. However, being a dream-maker also calls for raising our consciousness in the way we perceive life and go about manifesting experiences.

To fully leverage our capacity to imagine and realize possibilities, we need to awaken to how much beauty, wonder and grace is *already* in and around us every day. This state of being does not require us to do anything but to pause long enough from our day-to-day busyness and pay attention.

By activating a conscious intention to celebrate for any or no reason, we build a habit of appreciation and gratitude for our lives at this very moment, regardless of the circumstances. After all, we create from the here and now. If we turn away from our path, from where do we create our future?

It is as Oprah observed, the more we acknowledge the good in our lives and rejoice in our good fortune, the more we tune our radio receiver to attract more good fortune. By praising and celebrating any and all that is good in our lives – even just the great cup of tea we just enjoyed, or the crisp, fresh air after a cleansing rainstorm – we set our radio tuner to receive things that generate even more good feelings.

Celebration keeps the circulation of good going, reminds us of how blessed we are, and trains our subconscious to recognize the progress we are making toward the life of our dreams. It is one of the key components of the REACH roadmap.

This chapter is devoted to looking at the amazing power of celebration. We will talk about celebrating life in general and the inspired actions we take toward realizing our dreams, including the progress we make in our SMART plan from Chapter 4 - Act. We will also look at how we can choose to live in a state of grace by cultivating a consciousness of appreciation and gratitude. And, yes, we will discuss celebrating *you*, as your very existence is valuable to the people you already touched and have yet to touch.

The Amazing Energy of Celebration

In 2010, the San Francisco Giants won the World Series for the first time since the team moved from New York in 1954. To say that I am not a baseball fan is an understatement. I hardly know anything about the game, but have gone to a Giants game years ago, and thought it was great fun.

Even though I could barely follow the game much of the time, I loved being part of the energy of a stadium full of fans rooting for the home team. When a player came up to bat, his own special song would be played just for him, joined by the cheering of the fans. There was something really special about being part of such collective, vibrant energy. It is indescribable.

Back to the 2010 World Series, there was a victory parade going through the City – what the locals call San Francisco. At the time, my consulting work took me to the Financial District in the City, and the victory parade was to pass right by the block where I worked. It was history making right in front of my eyes, and I had to be part of the celebration.

So, I joined an excited crowd of spectators, as street car after street car of players passed by, greeted by thunderous cheering and applause by residents from all over the San Francisco Bay Area, business professionals and tourists alike. Probably just like me, many of the spectators had never seen or heard of these players, but it mattered not one bit.

The celebratory energy was so high and so enormous that I felt it connecting me to the tens of thousands of people witnessing history being made. In that stretch of time, it felt like *anything* was possible. Even now, as I attempt to recount that scene, I feel that words truly fail to convey the enormity of the energy of which I was a part. My heart is expanded just recalling that event, and my eyes are welling up.

That experience was such a powerful testament to the power of celebration. It was more than just the obvious, i.e., the historic victory of the home team. Above and beyond that, what captured my attention, too, were the deeper layers of meaning and significance that came with this piece of history.

This parade happened during what we now look back and call the Great Recession. With the mortgage industry woes and the collapse of giants in the financial services sector, jobs were lost, lives were affected, and local businesses suffered the second-order effects of seeing fewer patrons and less income. The prevailing energy was one of fear, struggle, desperation and the question of "When are things gonna look up?"

I am sure that wherever you were in the U.S. during the time, you felt this energy more or less intensely, too. But, during the playoffs leading up to the World Series, business at local pubs and sports bars boomed as a result of the local team being poised to go to the World Series for the first time and then poised to win the World Series for the first time. There was an energy of hope, excitement and anticipation that distracted the fans from the ongoing woes about the economy, even if just for a few moments at a time.

On the day of the parade, public transit systems – buses, ferries and trains – were grossly unprepared for the exponential increase in ridership they were not at all scaled to serve. Yet, in the presence of unprecedented masses, order was maintained. Long lines of passengers waited for their turns, and everything went smoothly even through delays and extremely packed vessels.

The massive crowds overwhelmed the normal service procedures of the regional subway system. Continuing to charge fare simply would have created too much slowdown in moving passengers through, and many would be sure to miss the parade. So, the transit authority soon adapted to the situation, and decided to give free rides into the City.

Moreover, immediately after the parade, the City of San Francisco's Public Works Department was right on scene to clean up the massive amounts of confetti left on the streets surrounding the parade route. These public servants did an amazing job with impressive efficiency. Within a couple of hours, there was no sign of any litter left by tens of thousands of excited spectators, who gathered to witness a great historic celebration.

I am gushing about this event, because it so perfectly illustrates the power of being in celebration. When we have something celebratory on which to focus, it takes our energy to a higher level, regardless of what else objectively is going on in our lives. Those who were down and scared about the economy set aside their fears one pitch at a time during the playoffs and the World Series, and then for the good part of a day to celebrate. Public service professionals were swept up in the energy, too, and did what was right for the occasion.

Obviously, the home team does not win the World Series every day, nor does it take a historic victory parade for us to activate the energy of celebration. While it is certainly easier for big events to inspire us to feel celebratory, we can *choose* to activate celebratory energy anytime, anywhere – just like my friend and I did after the workshop we attended.

When we focus our attention on reasons to celebrate, no matter what they are, we divert our attention away from the less ideal circumstances of our lives. Focusing on reasons to celebrate creates an amazing energy field that elevates our vibration. That, in turn, attracts better-feeling experiences with matching frequencies. Isn't that worth cultivating some consciousness and practice?

O *Contemplation Exercise*

- Bring yourself back to a celebratory moment in your life, whether it was big or small. How did it feel?
- How does this trip down memory lane feel? Wouldn't you like to have the same feeling more of the time?

Importance of Celebrating Successes

If you are like me, you build your life around setting goals and working tirelessly to achieve them. Each time you get to the finish line of a goal, you may allow yourself to feel a sense of accomplishment momentarily. But it is done, and you are onto your next goal. You are negligent about acknowledging your achievements and celebrating the wins. Instead, you only notice when you fail to do something or to do it well, no matter how much you tried or what else you have done in the meantime. You persistently focus only on the proverbial hole in the donut, and inadvertently perpetuate the negativity bias in your subconscious. Does this sound familiar?

A few years back, I was at a workshop that validated the importance of celebrating successes, giving ourselves due recognition for progress made toward a long-term goal. What was quite interesting was that most of us – all women – thought we did not have much to celebrate. We were really hard on ourselves because our career, love life, financial situation, and so forth, were not where we would like these areas of our lives to be.

But, once we started taking stock of what we did in the previous year, it became very evident that we *had* indeed made progress toward the lives we wanted, that there *were* reasons to celebrate. The actions took courage, commitment and devotion, among other things. These signs of progress should not be overlooked. It is critical to acknowledge and celebrate them.

While glossing over achievements leads to taking things for granted, celebration recognizes what we are able to manifest in our lives. Celebrating our achievements activates recognition of *ourselves* for being the powerful creators we are, training our subconscious to register evidence of progress. It makes us feel good and motivated to soldier on toward the life of our dreams.

If you are looking to transform your life, you know that it is not a five-day endeavor, but more likely something that will stretch over a longer period of time. It is critical that you notice and appreciate your progress regularly, lest you get discouraged. You want to stay motivated and excited about the long-term goal as you stride forward one step at a time.

Celebration signals to your subconscious – and your inner critic – that you are thankful for the progress you are making toward your dream. Most importantly, it allows you to stay in the flow of joy and expansion. *Look what I have accomplished!*

When I say celebrate, it can be anything that is meaningful to you. It can be something big, like taking yourself on your dream vacation. I know someone who would think about how she would celebrate a major achievement by taking herself to Europe. This keeps her motivated to get her work done. And the work ultimately puts her on her path towards her life purpose. It is a total win-win.

I have another friend who is the quintessential athlete. Staying fit and living a physically healthy life is vital to her. So, one of the ways she celebrates is to allow herself a whole day of exercise without interruption. While working out does not seem like much of a celebration to many – myself included – it is personally meaningful to her, and that is the only thing that matters.

If you tend to get discouraged easily, it is that much more important for you to take the time to celebrate any progress you have made. Treat yourself to a spa day. Reward yourself with a nice new putter employing state-of-the-art technology. Have a movie day with your favorite films, along with takeout food from your favorite restaurant, and do nothing else.

Schedule a celebration with a friend or a loved one. That would actually give you an extra incentive to make progress, as you do not want to have to cancel plans on someone else. It is a very positive way to hold yourself accountable for taking action. Besides, as social creatures, we thrive on interpersonal connections and the nurturing we get from healthy, loving and supportive relationships.

When you celebrate with loved ones, not only do you get the benefit of riding on the high of accomplishing a goal, you get the double benefit of basking in the energy of those around you who feel happy for you. What is more, your success may inspire them, too.

In any event, whatever gives you pleasure and marks the occasion in a meaningful way for you makes for a good celebration.

In case you are feeling some resistance to celebrating your progress or accomplishments, let me offer the following thoughts. I have learned that giving achievements – big or small – and good-faith effort due recognition is neither indulgent nor narcissistic. It is necessary for realizing our dreams. Doing so registers in our subconscious the good things we have done, not just what we have failed to do.

When we neglect to acknowledge and celebrate what deserves recognition, we run the risk of taking things for granted and minimizing how powerful we are in creating our own destiny. Instead, we unknowingly trap ourselves in a consciousness of lack, struggle and/or victimhood, that life is hard and full of hurdles. We wonder why that job, that relationship, or whatever it is that we want still has not shown up, even though many good things have already manifested – but we have completely taken them for granted.

By celebrating where we are and what we have already done, we open ourselves up to more, and we make ourselves magnetic to our dreams.

○ *Contemplation Exercise*

- Take out the SMART plan you started working on in the *Act* chapter, and review each of the goals you have set for yourself.
- Think about how you would like to celebrate each accomplished goal. Write these celebration plans down in your SMART plan, and commit to carrying them out. Start scheduling your celebrations!

As I mentioned in the last chapter, I created a SMART plan for writing this book. After each finished chapter, I celebrated the milestone. After completing one chapter, I had a nice, leisurely dinner with a friend. For another, I went out to high tea with two other friends. Rest assured, I will be celebrating the completion of this book!

Quite simply, when we pause to celebrate the progress we are making toward our dreams, we cultivate a new habit to increase our consciousness. From the Abraham-Hicks workshop I mentioned at the start of this chapter, when we link up the improvements in our lives with the good feelings of having achieved these results, we build new "thought-ways" for getting into the vortex. That is, we drop old thought patterns and establish new ones that get us closer to being in alignment with our desires.

Expressed differently, by consciously acknowledging what we have achieved, whether in releasing old beliefs or achieving a SMART goal, we reveal to our subconscious mind more of the path ahead of us that will take us to our dreams. Therefore, achieving any SMART goal – no matter how small it is – is a good reason to celebrate.

Choosing to Live in a State of Grace

My day begins with my morning spiritual practice, which consists of journaling, meditation, stretching and prayer. With rare exceptions, I keep to this daily practice, because it keeps me connected to my inner wisdom and grounded in the consciousness that how I perceive things generates the experience. That is, if I expect my day to go well, I will notice all the things that do go well. If I fear that the sky would fall, then it will undoubtedly be one fire drill after another. I *always* get to be right.

As my consciousness increases with continuing spiritual study and practice, I realize more and more that choosing to live in a state of grace is the best way to ensure that my day goes harmoniously and joyfully.

In *Thanks! How the New Science of Gratitude Can Make You Happier*, Dr. Robert Emmons talks about grace as the presence of goodness in our lives that exists independent of what we do or exceeding what our efforts merit. In other words, grace is a free gift to us. When we embrace grace in the world, it is easier for us to appreciate the "bonuses" in our lives, since we did not earn them. However, it is challenging for most of us to perceive grace (pg. 8):

> "The human mind contains mental tools that appear to work against the tendency to perceive grace. We are forgetful. We take things for granted. We have high expectations. We assume that we are totally responsible for all the good that comes our way. After all, we have earned it. We deserve it."

Perceiving grace, like all other observations we make in life, is a matter of choice. Unless we make a point of paying attention to the gifts of grace bestowed upon us, we unconsciously take them for granted – just like we take for granted things that go well for us, when we do not pause to acknowledge and celebrate them.

On a Monday morning a few months ago, I dreaded the work day because of a problematic project at work. I did not want to face what might be awaiting me at the office. I wanted to shift my energy and focus from that of dread to grace.

So, for the entire 50 minutes on my commute, I engaged in continuous bursts of appreciation. I said aloud anything that came to mind or came into sight which inspired appreciation – from my lovely home, to the great car I was driving, to the trees I passed along the way, to all the faces of people who came into mind. That went on for 50 minutes without stopping.

By the time I reached work, I was in such a state of grace, riding on such high, appreciative energy that I felt I could face anything. And, my day went really smoothly. In fact, it ended with my business partners expressing gratitude to me for going out of my way to make them feel comfortable about the objectively problematic situation.

If I had stewed in all the scenarios of what further might go wrong with this project for the same 50 minutes, I would have been a total nervous wreck by the time I got into work. I would have gone into the meeting with my business partners ready to fight fire – and inadvertently looking for confirmation that more problems were on the horizon. It certainly would not have ended with gratitude expressed.

Can you see the difference between the two scenarios? By approaching life from a mindset of grace, we can shift our consciousness and where we focus our attention and energy. By taking note of what feels good in our lives, no matter how insignificant the objects of appreciation may seem, we avoid creating self-fulfilling prophecies in negative experiences.

Don't think that shifting your energy means having to look for the good in an objectively challenging situation while you are in the middle of it. Obviously, if you are able to do that, you will have an easier time getting through it. Short of that, just focusing your attention away from the troubling situation to *anything* that makes you feel good is an effective tactic. It not only gives yourself some relief, it also serves to activate a state of grace.

Have you ever experienced even a brief moment when everything just seems to flow? It may be that you noticed the sun shining on a lazy Sunday morning, or the raindrops from a tree branch in your backyard looking like diamonds. Or, you were on the floor with your kids playing, and their unabashed joy simply filled your heart. In that moment, you had exactly what you wanted, and you were exactly where you wanted to be – all without any effort. These are moments of grace, and we all have them – if we pay attention.

If you cannot think of any, it is likely that you forgot or your attention was focused elsewhere. Practice paying attention. Try to notice as often as you can the little delights in your life, whatever they are. You may be driving home from work, relieved that the work day is over. Pay attention to a tree or a billboard you pass on the way home, or a new car passing you that catches your eye.

When you start noticing these little things in your environment, you can build on that and expand your consciousness of grace in your life. You will start to sharpen your intention to focus on that which pleases you and away from whatever the stress of the day happens to be.

○ *Contemplation Exercise*

- Block out 5 minutes in your calendar for each day over the next 21 days. (Again, that is how long it takes to create a new habit.)

- During those 5 minutes, pay attention to your surroundings, and notice everything you appreciate, whether it is a cup, a bird that flies by outside your window, or the voices of kids having fun in a nearby playground.

- Feel free to incorporate these 5 minutes into other things that you do, such as taking a walk, commuting or grocery shopping. Whatever you do, be sure you pay attention and feel appreciation for the things around you.

- Try to journal on your daily reactions but most certainly at the end of each week. What did you notice about any changes in your consciousness? What did you notice that you might otherwise have taken for granted? How did it feel to be consciously noticing things to appreciate?

The other day, I was very much loving the creative flow in my writing, feeling really connected to source energy. I took a walk to stretch my legs and to get my blood circulating. It was early February, and technically it was still winter. Yet, the temperature was in the 70s, and the sun was shining brilliantly. It was the perfect Sunday afternoon to take a walk around my neighborhood.

As I walked, I noticed the different trees, and how they all stood so differently, extending their branches in every which way, some gracefully, some expressively, some majestically. The leaves were of different shapes, sizes and colors, and they stood at different heights.

As I admired the handy work of Mother Nature, I heard the melodious songs of birds over head. I could not see them, but I heard them from way deep in my heart and soul. In those 30 minutes, I was in total bliss! I was fully basking in a state of grace.

Over time, I have had similar experiences when I go out to commune with nature, even though I really do not consider myself a nature buff. As Dr. Deepak Chopra says, when we are out in nature, the rhythm of our bodies gets synchronized to that of Mother Earth. That is one of the reasons why we often feel a higher state of wellbeing after a hike or a trip to the woods or the ocean.

A favorite spot close to home is a reservoir. There, I see the perfect blend of nature at its best – clear water that looks like crystals when light hits its surface. On a sunny day, the water shimmers like a gigantic sheet of glimmer glass. It is breathtakingly beautiful! All this is accompanied by mountains in the backdrop with evergreen trees.

One time, when I was there and appreciating the majestic sight I was beholding, I swear that the trees at a distance swayed back and forth – on a calm day without winds – just to greet me. Those moments of communion with nature brought me so close to the source of everything on Earth. In those moments, I was one with the beauty of nature, one with the pulse of the energy that created and sustains worlds and lives.

That is the ultimate state of grace, the ultimate reason to celebrate life just because. I did not win the lottery, nor did I fall in love, at least not with another human being. I felt blissful for no other reason than I just was.

Perhaps you have an affinity to nature, perhaps not. Whether or not you do, when you are out and about – whether around your neighborhood or traveling on a tree-lined street – pay attention to the things that are not fabricated by human beings. Take note of whether noticing these specimens of nature evokes calmness, tranquility or peace within you, even if just for a brief moment. This brief moment is one in the state of grace.

Cultivating a Habit of Appreciation and Gratitude

In *Thanks!*, Dr. Emmons details research findings about the many benefits of gratitude – including its connection to happiness, health, resilience and longevity, just to name a few.

He also links gratitude directly to grace, which we just discussed. Specifically, grateful people are more ready to take note of goodness in their lives that have nothing to do with them. In other words, when we are in gratitude, we are more inclined to recognize grace. Furthermore, just like perceiving grace is a conscious choice, being in gratitude also takes conscious practice.

Even if you have not read *Thanks!*, I am quite sure that you have heard from different sources how important it is to have an attitude of gratitude. When you take stock of what you have and how truly grateful you are for the many blessings in your life, your heart space and gratitude consciousness expand. You vibrate at a frequency that attracts more of what you want.

On the contrary, when you dwell on the negative emotions of what is not going well in your life, and concentrate on the lack of what you want, you ask the universe to respond to your negative state all the same.

The universe does not judge whether your vibrational offerings are positive or negative. It takes these requests as they are without any interpretation of good or bad. The sole job of your cosmic manifestation partner is to deliver to you what you request through the energy you put out, the frequencies of your beliefs, as expressed through your thoughts and feelings.

So, one good way to ensure that you are tuned into receiving what you want is to be in a positive state of expectancy and anticipation. Nothing puts you there quite like being in appreciation and gratitude.

Appreciation

Appreciation and gratitude are very similar in that they both activate good feelings based on our observation of the source of such positive emotions, whether it is a person, an object or an event.

Perhaps, it may seem like splitting hairs, but the subtle difference between the two is that gratitude is often inspired by receiving something, such as a gift, a compliment or an act of service. Appreciation, on the other hand, is not conditioned upon receiving anything, nor does the object being appreciated expect anything in return.

My experience connecting with nature right in my backyard is an example of being in appreciation. My continuous bursts of appreciation on my 50-minute commute represent another example. In both cases, no one gave me anything, and I certainly was not saying "Thank You" to anyone in particular, although I felt grateful. More importantly, though, my appreciation consciousness was turned on.

For an exquisite description of appreciation, read the following beautiful passage from *What Happy People Know*, by Dan Baker and Cameron Stauth (pg. 81):

> "Appreciation is the highest and purest form of love. It is the outward-bound, self-renewing form of love that has no dependence upon romantic attachment or family ties. People who truly appreciate feel the same about the object of their appreciation whether

it is present or absent. They appreciate even if it is, by objective standards, not worthy of their appreciation. Appreciation asks for nothing, and gives everything.

When you enter into the active condition of appreciation—whether over something as common as a sunset or as profound as the love in your child's eyes—your normal world stops and a state of grace begins. Time can stand still, or rush like a waterfall. Your senses are heightened or obliterated. Creativity flows, heart rate slows, brain waves soften into rolling ripples, and an exquisite calm descends over your entire being. During active appreciation, your brain, heart and endocrine system work in synchrony and heal in harmony."

Are you as moved by the imagery depicted in the above passage as I am? Don't you just want to savor the deliciousness of feeling this great as often as possible?

Since it is entirely up to us to *choose* to be in a state of appreciation, to look for things to appreciate, we can bask in this exquisite state of grace as often as we want, for as long as we want. We do not need anyone's approval or participation to experience it. All we need to do is to *choose* to notice that which pleases us and inspires us to step through the gates of appreciation. When we enter those gates often, we celebrate life just as it is. That is why, as an agent of celebration, appreciation is a wonderful companion on our road to realizing our dreams.

Gratitude

Aside from being in an active state of appreciation, another way to celebrate life is to cultivate a gratitude consciousness for what we already have in our life right now that is good.

Some of you may think, "*Whoa! I don't want more of my life! I want to change it for the better, not create more of the same.*" Note that I am recommending that you focus on the positive things in your life, not the negative conditions. This is not about discounting real life challenges. It is about placing your conscious attention on the parts that good, lest you take them for granted.

If you are really down in your luck, count the blessings you do have; everyone has at least some. Be grateful for the fact that you have the gift of your eyesight to be able to read this book. Be grateful that you know how to read. Not everyone has these blessings. Be grateful for how your morning cup of coffee invigorates you and how the aroma delights you – that you are blessed with the senses of taste and smell. Again, not everyone is so lucky. These are good places to start.

Cultivate a consciousness of paying attention to what is good in your life, no matter how small you think they are. For instance, next time someone says "Thank You" to you or pays you a compliment, really let those words sink in, rather than treat them as rhetorical speech. Be grateful for them. Celebrate them. Watch your consciousness gradually expand to notice more good.

O *Contemplation Exercise*

To demonstrate how being in a state of gratitude shifts your energy away from negative thoughts, let's do a very simple exercise.

- Close your eyes and think of someone or something you are thankful for in your life. For a couple of minutes, just keep seeing this person or event. Notice what s/he is doing, saying to you. Notice what is happening.

- How does it feel in your body? Do you feel warm and expanded? Is there any room for negative thought?

- Now, for the next couple of minutes, think of someone or something that brings you stress or grief of any kind. Notice what s/he is doing, saying to you. Notice what is happening.

- How does that feel in your body? Do you feel your heart contracting, your body tensing up?

How was the exercise for you? Did you notice the differences in the two simple recalls and how differently they feel in your body? If you have a choice, which set of feelings would you rather have more of the time? And, guess what? You *do* have that choice.

You do not have to be in denial about the challenging circumstances in your life. In fact, it is unhealthy to suppress your feelings. After all, the energy you put into pushing these feelings away comes with an equally powerful reactive force that shows up in a corresponding experience. You now know tools from the *Release* chapter to process and let go of any negativity – use them.

By *consciously choosing* to be in gratitude, by focusing on the thoughts that lead to expansion in your chest rather than contraction, by choosing feelings of ease instead of tension, you are doing yourself a huge favor. By choosing to feel good, you tune your radio to the frequencies of receiving good. By being in gratitude, even when your life circumstances are not ideal, you are choosing to shift your energy to welcome more things to come that create more of these good feelings, more reasons to celebrate. The universe then conspires to line up the external circumstances of your life to match what you seek, based on your internal state.

As a practice to cultivate your gratitude consciousness, I highly recommend that you keep a gratitude journal. It does not have to take a lot of time, and you can do it right before you go to sleep. List the things for which you are grateful for each day, no matter how insignificant they may seem objectively. Try to do it for 21 days straight, as the practice will have a better chance of sticking as a habit.

Since a few years ago, I have been keeping a nightly gratitude journal myself. As a result of this daily practice that takes only a few minutes each evening, my gratitude for all the blessings in my life has grown. Along with appreciation for the little things in my world – such as birdsong and interesting trees I notice all the time – I have expanded my capacity to choose more often to live in a state of grace.

Celebrating You

I realize that this subtitle may make some of you uneasy, but a discussion of celebrating life is simply incomplete without talking about the star of the show. Trust me, I would not have been comfortable either with the idea of celebrating myself even a few short years ago. *Celebrate me? What is there to celebrate?* But, the truth for all of us, without exception, is that our very existence has already touched the lives of many, and will touch those of many others.

I am not talking about the future improved you, once you will have made whatever changes you deem are necessary for you to be worthy of celebration. I mean the you right now, just as you are, no tweaking, no major overhaul. If you have a difficult time with this idea, do not despair, you are not alone. Keep an open mind for now and keep reading. If you still find it troubling, you can skip the contemplation exercise at the end. You will also find the next chapter, *Honor*, to be comforting.

Have you ever watched the classic Holiday movie, *It's A Wonderful Life*? Think about George Bailey and how objectively desperate his situation is. He thinks he has nothing to live for anymore, until his guardian angel, Clarence, opens his eyes to what the lives of his loved ones would be like if he weren't around.

Alice P. Chan, Ph.D.

Even though this is just a movie, the message is very applicable to real life. We can get so caught up in the circumstances of our lives that we forget how valuable we are. Until we take a step back to consider how interconnected we are with others, we can grossly underestimate the value of our existence, the value of *us*.

When I think of my adult life now with the benefit of hindsight, I can see clearly the progression of growth through the decades, and how each was necessary on my life path. Perhaps some of this may resonate with you.

I see my 20s as a decade of trying to find myself through trial and error, trying to establish my self-worth and identity through blind achievements. Attempts to source my value as a person through my professional identity and accomplishments continued well into my 30s. I came into my own in my 40s. (When this book was first written in 2011, I was in my early 40s.)

Now in my 50s, I am celebrating a sense of freedom to be that I did not feel in my younger days. I am proud and humbled to be the woman I have become. I am proud because of how much I have grown and transformed, knowing that I will continue to grow and transform until it is time to surrender this human body. I feel humbled by the honor and privilege to have experienced so much richness in just a little over five decades of living – including through a once-in-a-century pandemic that is still in process as of the writing of this 2021 update.

In celebrating who I have become, I do not think I am perfect, far from it. Instead, I have grown comfortable in my own skin, with my strengths and weaknesses happily cohabitating. In counting my blessings, I am grateful for not just the gifts bestowed upon me to create in this life, but also my vulnerabilities.

Whereas once I was afraid to appear weak, and I would do anything to hide my vulnerabilities, I now see them as indispensable parts of me. They add authenticity to my writing, speaking and teaching voice, reminding me to speak from my heart, not just from my intellect. They power my compassionate spirit to relate at a deep level to others who are lost and/or afraid – because I know firsthand what that feels like.

With all that said, I feel privileged to have this life, and would not want to be anyone else but me – in this precise package, on this precise path. And, with gratitude, I celebrate the woman I am today!

What about you? Are you ready to celebrate you? If you feel that you have nothing to celebrate, try asking loved ones what they would celebrate about you. Have you ever participated in an exercise when people write on a sheet of paper posted on your back as to what they appreciate about you? Yes, you quite literally get to know what they say about you behind your back!

I had such an experience twice over the years, and it was quite eye-opening how I did not see what others saw. So, try that. You do not have to have people literally write on your back. But, ask your friends and family the qualities they value about you. At the minimum, think about what they might say if you were to ask them.

○ *Contemplation Exercise*
- Are you ready to celebrate you? Why or why not?

If you are not ready to celebrate you, know that it is perfectly ok. This exercise is intended to build some baseline awareness. As you will see in the next chapter, *Honor*, no matter what you are or are not ready to do, you are ok.

As closing thoughts for this chapter, let me offer two recommendations about keeping celebration front and center in your consciousness.

Alice P. Chan, Ph.D.

First, it is always a matter of choice for all of us to live in a state of grace as often as we want and for as long as we want. And we enter this state of grace through a conscious practice of appreciation and gratitude.

As for the second thought, when we choose to celebrate life, life in turn celebrates us. We always get back what we energetically offer. So, rather than wait for a reason to celebrate, celebrate the reason into existence. Do that by celebrating yourself, as well as your achievements and progress, and by cultivating a habit of appreciation and gratitude for the people and things in your world.

Happy Celebrating!

Summary Points for Celebrate

- Celebration keeps the circulation of good going, and reminds us of how blessed we are.

- Cultivate a habit of celebrating for any and all reasons – or no reason at all – not just major achievements or occasions. Celebration takes us to a higher energy level, regardless of what else objectively is going on in our lives.

- Celebrating each step of our achievements activates recognition of ourselves for being the powerful creators we are. It makes us feel good and motivated to soldier on toward the life of our dreams.

- Celebrations can be big or small, but make them personally meaningful to you. Celebrating with loved ones is a great idea, as it allows you to share in the high energy of accomplishing a goal with someone who feels happy for you. It also is a positive way to hold yourself accountable to avoid canceling plans with someone else.

- Add celebrations to your in-progress SMART Plan from Chapter 4 – Act.

- Choosing to live in a state of grace is the best way to ensure that your consciousness is focused on celebration. And you can enter that state by conscious practice of appreciation and gratitude. Practice noticing things in your everyday life that inspire appreciation, no matter how small or insignificant they may appear to you. Take stock of what you have in your life for which to be grateful. Keep a gratitude journal.

- Your very existence is a reason to celebrate. If you find it challenging to know what to celebrate about yourself, ask friends and family what they value about you.

- Cultivate your celebration consciousness. Choose to celebrate life, and life will celebrate you in return.

CHAPTER 6

Honor

"Nothing that you have ever done or will ever do can mar your perfection ... What you do or don't do is not what determines your value—your growth perhaps, but not your value."
— Marianne Williamson

In the full text of the above quote, the first sentence actually ends with "in the eyes of God." I deliberately took this last phrase out to show you that, whether you actually believe in a higher power, the fundamental truth about you remains the same.

This quote is from one of my all-time favorite books, *A Return to Love*, by Marianne Williamson. For those of you who have read her work or heard her speak, you will agree that she is one of our greatest contemporary teachers of spirituality and unconditional love.

When we are unable to accept and love ourselves just as we are, just where we are in our lives, we judge ourselves for a myriad of failures and inadequacies – such as, not knowing what we want, not doing enough, not having the courage and tenacity to stick with any change we want to make in our lives. Do any of these sound familiar to you?

This advice from Williamson is very much aligned with my REACH philosophy. As we take steps toward realizing our dreams, it is a good reminder to recognize that our inherent value does not stem from our actions. No matter what we do or not, it may say something about how we fare relative to achieving our dreams or our readiness to better our lives.

However, while achieving goals may lead to more success and satisfaction – which is superb! – taking action, in and of itself, does not make us inherently more worthy. In the same vein, not doing something does not diminish our intrinsic value or make us a failure in the grand scheme of life. Recognize that it is our ego's specialty to be quick and masterful at labeling us based on our action or inaction.

The truth is that we are who we are, *not* what we do or what we fail to do. If we are willing to accept this truth about ourselves, we learn to ease the pressure we feel to behave in a certain way in order to gain approval and acceptance from others. We learn to choose what to do because it makes us feel good – including fulfilling our dreams – not because we have to do them to be worthy. In time, we will realize that life is full of grace, joy and freedom.

Cultivating this consciousness – to realize our inherent worth, instead of sourcing it from our actions to seek external validation – is the essence of what honoring ourselves and our life path is all about.

With the above said, this chapter is devoted to helping us maintain perspective on all that we have been doing – and will continue to do – to REACH our dreams. After all, we create from where we are, what we have, and who we believe ourselves to be at any given moment. Any desired change or improvement starts with the here and now.

By honoring who we are, including our body, and where we are on our path at the present time, we honor the creative capacities from which to manifest our dreams. We will talk about all that in the coming pages.

We will also look at things that are challenging to honor at face value, but are nonetheless important to recognize and appreciate. After all, we are quite likely to run into them again on the path to our dreams. These include: (1) the mystery of timing – why it is often a gift that things do not happen as fast as we want, or not at all; (2) the gift of distractions – judgments of having veered off our path; and (3) people we encounter on our path.

We will wrap up this chapter by looking at honoring our life path by doing what is ours to do and surrendering control of the rest.

Honor Who You are, With No Strings Attached

In Marci Shimoff's book, *Love for No Reason*, one of the many insights she shared is that most of us harbor some version of "not good enough" – not special enough, not valuable enough, not smart enough, not attractive enough, not creative enough, and so on. Perhaps some of these ring true for you.

Much of what blocks our good from coming into our lives stems from this family of limiting self-perceptions. We have somehow internalized the belief that we do not deserve more than our current lot, unless we "fix" ourselves in one way or more.

As we covered earlier in this book, we usually unknowingly acquired these perceptions at a very young age. Such seeds of inadequacy and lack of self-worth took root in the fertile soil of our unsophisticated, impressionable young minds. Over time, they grow into full-blown self-limiting beliefs, when we experience again and again the yearning to be accepted and loved, only to feel over and over again that we seemingly have to *qualify for* it.

For some of us, that qualification for acceptance and love may be internalized as the need to be perfect always. There is no room for the slightest margin for error. Or it may be not feeling ok to say "no," to have boundaries, for fear we would be deemed selfish and be rejected. It may be feeling pressured to conform to a set of prescribed behavior we abhor. It may be feeling that our lovability rises and falls with perceived competency, that not knowing something we think we should know somehow diminishes our right to breathe.

There are many variations to what qualifying for love looks like. Regardless of how we learned to seek acceptance and love outside ourselves, we feel unworthy of it until we fulfill the conditions to *earn* them.

When we attempt to earn acceptance and love from others, we inadvertently wait for them to fill our love reservoir. When that happens, we give away our personal power. What I mean by giving away power is that we let someone else determine how valuable and lovable we are. Think about how powerful that makes them, and how much that diminishes our own power.

If you have the choice to (re)claim that power to determine your own value, wouldn't you want to do that? And, guess what? You most certainly have that choice!

We ourselves hold the richest supply of love for our inner reservoir. This self-generating love will power up our dream engine, and provide the ever-renewing energy for taking guided action. This love has no strings attached, nor does it need to be earned. It is where we come from, and with which each and every one of us was born – without exception.

If we have trouble believing that, we simply have not learned our true nature. Instead, the truth of who we are is buried under layers of life experiences. Subconsciously, those experiences trained us to believe that love does not come easily.

In order to create expansiveness in our lives for our dreams to manifest, our inner love calls us to emerge from any cumulative rubbles of disappointments and accept ourselves – without judgment, without conditions. If this sounds like a tall order to you right now, just be *willing* to be open to this possibly being your truth. Know that it is perfectly ok if you are not in that place just yet.

This is the over-arching essence of honoring who you are. Honoring yourself does not require you to have reached whatever bar you believe you need to reach before feeling deserving. It starts with acknowledging who you are right now, independent of the objective circumstances of your life.

Please know that honoring yourself does not mean you should become Pollyanna, vacantly affirming that you are great, when you do not believe it for one second. What it does mean, however, is for you to believe that the current version of you – without "fixing" – is good enough. Otherwise, attempting to follow this REACH program will become yet another potential reason to feel guilty, to feel like a failure – when your ego gets in your face for daring to dream beyond your comfort zone, or if you should miss a SMART goal.

If you have ever attempted to set New Year's resolutions – only to have them fall on the wayside before the first quarter of the year is up – you know what I mean. You end up not changing what you set out to change and continuing to feel crummy about the unchanged condition. On top of that, you now feel even worse because of the additional self-indictment of not having followed through. Let's not repeat this double whammy.

This is why *"Honor"* is a crucial component of REACH. Hone your ability to honor the current version of you, you honor your right to dream, without having to qualify for the privilege. In turn, the portal to the juiciest inner dream will open before you.

○ *Contemplation Exercise*

- Despite whatever ways you feel you are not good enough, are you ready to honor the fact that you are ok just the way you are, without any need to be "fixed"? If not:
    - What is holding you back? Are you open to the possibility of this thought being true, that the current you is ok?

- Consider going back to the *Release* chapter to let go of the barriers that came up.
- Think of someone who truly loves you, including the higher power of your understanding. What would they say about honoring you just the way you are?

Honor Your Body

We cannot leave the topic of honoring you without talking about honoring your body. You probably think this section is a call for you to maintain a healthy diet, exercise, get sufficient rest, and take care of your overall physical health.

I do indeed urge you to do all that, as your body is the physical apparatus through which you create and enjoy the fruits of your creation. However, honoring your body goes beyond taking care of your physical health. It involves honoring – and listening to – the wisdom coming through your body.

Our body holds a tremendous amount of intuitive intelligence, and it always knows what is for our highest good. Physical sensations we normally do not notice or take for granted actually contain a great deal of wisdom about our well being.

In *Power, Freedom and Grace*, Dr. Deepak Chopra says that, when we listen to our body, we access the intuitive intelligence within us that is more accurate and precise than our rational thought. He further explains (pg. 193):

> "When confronted with any situation, ask your body whether it feels comfortable or not. If the sensation in your body feels good when you do something, then that's the right decision. If there's an uncomfortable sensation in your body, then it's not the right thing to do.

> When you are out of harmony with universal rhythms, the signal that will come to you is a sense of discomfort, whether it's physical, mental or emotional. When you are flowing in harmony with the universe, the signal that will come to you is a sense of comfort, ease, or joy."

Have you ever had an experience when your stomach – neck, shoulders, or some other body part – tightened about a decision you were facing, only to find out later that the physical sensation was a warning to you? That is an example of the intuitive intelligence within your body knowing that something was not for your highest good.

In my own experience, I had steered clear of a few men my gut told me I could not trust. There were no objective facts about why they were untrustworthy – at least not until *after* I had decided not to continue seeing them. By honoring the warning coming from my body's intuitive intelligence, I saved myself from serious heartbreak – or worse.

In *You Can Heal Your Life*, Louise Hay talks about the different messages we receive from different parts of our body. She provides a great, detailed taxonomy of what each of our body parts represents, and what a dis-ease associated with each signifies.

Notice that she purposely hyphenates "dis-ease" to isolate the root of "ease," which is our natural state – when we flow in harmony with universal rhythms and energy. When any part of our body does not function properly, it is because we are either resisting something or we are out of balance in some way. Recognizing that resistance or how we are out of balance, we can focus on shifting our beliefs about that specific area and affirm our truth instead.

In her taxonomy, she also provides targeted affirmations accordingly. You can also use the insights to practice Emotional Freedom Technique (EFT), which was introduced in the *Release* chapter.

As a case in point, you read a little earlier about the chronic eczema on my face. I looked up different things on the taxonomy and came up with an analysis that helped me to treat myself with EFT. Through chronic eczema on my face, the intuitive intelligence in my body was trying to get me to face – no pun intended – my fears about who I was meant to become. The collective message urged me to see that I was safe to be me, to express myself as a writer, speaker, teacher and coach, and that I was safe to embrace the future, to complete the life change I have felt called to make.

Until I fully committed to finishing this book and doing REACH work, the skin infection on my face – the chronic dis-ease – persisted to remind me to release all lingering fears and resistance to my calling.

In sum, honoring our body goes beyond taking care of our physical health. It involves getting in tune with the intuitive intelligence coming through our physical apparatus. It means paying attention to the messages our physical intuition sends us – whether it is a warning about a situation to avoid or a larger message about our inner dream. Whatever the message, it is ultimately for our highest good, and it would be wise for us to pay attention.

O *Contemplation Exercise*

- Recall a time when you faced a situation or decision, and you felt something in your body, whether a positive or negative sensation. Was it a warning or an encouragement?

- Did you follow that feeling in your decision or action? How did it turn out?

- Have you had a chronic physical condition, whether or not it is still on-going? What message do you think your body is/was trying to send you? You can consult *You Can Heal Your Life*.

We can tune into what we need in this life by following the intuitive guidance our body readily offers. Therefore, it is an excellent idea to cultivate a habit of paying attention to this intuitive intelligence. Next time you have a decision to make, remember to sit quietly and feel what physical sensations come to you. They are likely to contain wisdom about your impending decision.

Honor Where You Are in the Labyrinth of Life

As we covered at the start of our journey in this book, life is much more like a mysterious labyrinth than a straight path. Think about it, a big source of our angst and fears often stems from navigating a labyrinth. Sometimes, it feels like the center goal is literally within reach. But, somehow, the path starts taking us away from it. Other times, we feel utterly lost. These are the times when we really get discouraged.

Honoring where we are in the labyrinth of life is about trusting that the meandering path is guaranteed to get us to our goal, no matter how lost we may feel at any point. That is, if we have the faith and the endurance to stick it out, to keep saying "Yes" to taking the next step on our path.

For as long as I care to remember, I felt I had "accidentally" landed in my decade-plus business consulting career. I felt tremendous angst from seemingly having fallen off my life path. It did not match the psychological picture of the personally meaningful work I yearned to do. That was until I realized I was simply in the outer folds of the labyrinth of my life, far from the center goal of fulfilling my life purpose professionally.

It now makes perfect sense to me why my "accidental" consulting career was a crucial part of my journey. Among other things, it has helped me sharpen many skills that are extremely valuable to the REACH work I am called to do. While I continually dismissed the value of the consulting work I was doing, I was actually honing my skills and capacity to relate to those I was born to serve.

In the years I was busy judging myself for squandering my life, I was actually following an instinct since childhood. I thought I would grow up to be a helper of some sort. Therefore, my decade-long consulting career was anything but an accident. Being a consultant was an exact match to where I was: To help others by leveraging my formal education and professional experience.

I finally realized that the mounting angst I felt was from dishonoring my own life. After all, why would life honor me with pleasant and fulfilling experiences, when I had turned away from it and kept dismissing the value of my career opportunities – and the decisions and actions I took in response – along the way?

My example above serves to illustrate how deceptive the labyrinth of life can be – if we let our fear-based ego make sense of our life experiences, instead of trusting the wisdom of our inner compass to lead the way.

It is very tempting to misjudge being in the outer folds of our labyrinth as falling off our paths or taking detours. No matter how far it appears we have strayed away from the center goal, we are still somewhere *inside* our labyrinth, *on* our life path. What we choose to do, where we choose to turn at any point *always* fits into the grand scheme of our life.

When we are emotionally wedded to how things ought to look or how they need to play out, we miss the point of why we are where we are on our path. We inadvertently take for granted how valuable these "accidental" choices actually are, and how they are meant to prepare us for fulfilling our larger life purpose.

When viewed holistically from above, nothing looks out of place in the perfect and orderly circle of a labyrinth. Everything fits together in a unique pattern – the starting point, the windy path and the center goal. That unique pattern is the distinctiveness of your particular path. It is only when you lose sight of this holistic picture that self-judgment sets in and panic is triggered. Therefore, if you practice honoring where you are in the labyrinth of life, you practice having faith in your unique path, even if you cannot see immediately where it will take you.

○ *Contemplation Exercise*

- What have you done in your life that you feel are detours?
- What knowledge, skills or experiences have you gained from these seeming detours? How may they benefit who you want to be, what you want to do, or where you want to go ultimately?

In the labyrinth of life, there are no detours, nor can you fall off your path. No matter how lost you may feel, you are still very much *on* your path. Rather than fear the labyrinth and where you are in it, learn to see it as a game, a fun mystery to solve with deliberate choices you get to honor always.

Honor the Mystery of Timing

If you are like me, patience is less than a virtue, but rather something to cultivate consciously. When you really want something, you wanted it yesterday! It can be challenging to honor the time it takes for what you want to manifest. However, the bigger your dream, the more time it takes for the external circumstances of your life to line up. Besides, in the end, it will always become clear why the waiting is necessary.

In some cases, the waiting serves the critical purpose of signaling to you the presence of limiting beliefs blocking the way. After all, when what you want is delayed, it is often because you still unknowingly harbor contrary beliefs. If you still feel not good enough in any way – whether or not you are aware of it – you keep your dream at bay.

Regardless of how you overtly rationalize why you want what you want, unless the frequencies of your beliefs match those of your desires, you are essentially saying to the universe that you do not deserve the latter.

In other instances, the waiting helps you reassess your priorities and desires, which may change over time. While you are waiting for your dream to manifest, you may realize that you do not want what you *thought* you wanted after all. Whether it is a prestigious job, someone on whom you have had a long-time crush, or a specific place you want to call home, you may realize in time that this desire is ego-directed. Ultimately, having it will not fulfill you, and the wisest part of you knows that. It is simply waiting for you to come into this awareness.

You may have seen "The Last Lecture" that circulated on the Web in 2007. It was delivered by the late Randy Pausch, the inspiring Carnegie Mellon professor who died of pancreatic cancer at the tender age of 47 in 2008.

In his book with the same title, he talked about brick walls, especially the one associated with winning the heart of his wife. He said that brick walls are there to test how badly we really want something.

The waiting period for dreams to manifest is like an invisible brick wall. The bigger the dream, the longer it likely takes to gestate, and the bigger and thicker that brick wall may seem. If we end up waiting for a long time for something and still want it with all of our heart and soul, we must really want it, not just because it is simply fashionable or that we are expected to want it.

○ *Contemplation Exercise*

- Think of something you really wanted, which took a long time to materialize. What did you learn from the waiting period?

- Think of something else you thought you wanted. When you got it, you realized you did not want it after all. How did it help you redefine what you wanted instead?

When you feel impatient for something to happen, take a moment and remember to honor the mystery of timing. Aside from the fact that it takes time for cosmic forces to line up what you want, the waiting period may end up bearing incredible gifts to you.

Honor that there is a good reason – may be more than one – for why it is for your highest good to wait. Maybe you need to evolve your internal state more before you are a vibrational match to receive what you want. Maybe what you *thought* you wanted is no longer good for you, and you would be wise to redefine your dream.

As long as you are *willing* to honor the temporary discomfort of waiting, the right thing for you will come to you in due time. You simply *cannot* miss your life. Trust that, honor that, and the realization of the most beautiful dream is your prize at the end of the waiting.

Honor Distractions

In the *Act* chapter, we talked about anticipating distractions from taking action on our SMART goals. After all, we know that they are bound to come up; it is human nature to procrastinate on doing things that stretch our comfort. We also strategized on how to head them off as much as we can, so that they do not derail us completely from our plan.

It is clearly important that we are prepared for any and all distractions. But what happens when we *do* get distracted, despite the best of our preparation and intention? How do we put these distractions into perspective? What purpose do they serve other than to derail us?

Whether we are aware, distractions are direct consequences of the choices we make in life. They match our level of self-awareness and what we are ready to do. For those of us who find it challenging to follow through with our intentions and goals, distractions teach us to cultivate self-accountability, such as seeking help from trusted others.

Distractions also let us know that our goals may be too far of a stretch from our current circumstances and beliefs. As a result, we are more prone to accept the many procrastination excuses proffered by our ego to restore our comfort and safety. That is why we talked about being realistic with our dream action plan – the "R" in SMART.

Distractions can also serve as messengers about necessary changes we need to make in our lives. As discussed in the *Release* chapter, what we try to avoid indicates to us fears and old beliefs that need to go. When we feel distracted from doing something, pay attention to what we are trying to avoid and the underlying reasons. Chances are our inner wisdom is nudging us to change and grow.

Ultimately, distractions offer us opportunities to evaluate again and again how important our dream is to us, how much we truly want it. As you may have experienced before, when you felt a fire burning in your belly about something, and you simply could not imagine your world without it, nothing could stop you from going after it.

Similarly, when we are ready to embrace our dream as the highest priority in our lives, we find ourselves willing to commit to whatever it takes to make it a reality. Until we are truly ready though, distractions from our dream serve their purpose of keeping us honest.

Have you seen the movie, *Evan Almighty*? Evan is a senator called by God to build an arc right outside of Washington D.C. His wife thinks he has lost it, and proceeds to leave with the kids. While taking a food stop on their way to her parents' place, she encounters God.

God tells her that, when we pray for peace in our heart, God does not send us warm and fuzzy feelings. Instead, we are given opportunities to *choose* peace. When we pray for closeness in our family, God does not send us feelings of closeness. Rather, we are given opportunities to *choose* to be a close family.

The moral of the story is that it is Evan's wife's opportunity to *choose* what she claims she wants, i.e., to have a close family by supporting her husband at a time when he really needs her.

I'm bringing up this beautiful message from pop culture because of its tremendous wisdom. Even if you do not believe in God, when you claim you want something, be ready to walk the talk.

And, this message perfectly encapsulates why distractions in our lives are not to be shunned but honored. After all, they are direct results of our choices. We attract them into our lives to help us choose at every crossroads which way to go. If we are not ready for the tougher route, recognize that it is ok and honor that. Why beat ourselves up over not being ready for it? What purpose does chastising ourselves serve?

On the other hand, if we really want what we claim we want, then distractions are there to remind us that our choices and actions need to line up with our desires. It is what the late Pausch said about brick walls again. How badly do you want your dream? Are you willing to push through the brick wall of distractions to recommit to choices that align with your dream? Either way, it is the right answer. Just be deliberate with your choice and be ready to honor it – even if it means accepting temporary distractions and honoring their sacred place on your path.

○ *Contemplation Exercise*

- Think about where you are in your life right now and where you want to be. What are you doing now that distracts you from your dream?

- What purpose do you think these distractions serve?

Honor Others

For many of us, most of our waking hours are spent interacting with others – partners, colleagues, family, friends, and so on. Even when we are alone, some of that time is spent consciously or unconsciously processing those interactions, anticipating future encounters.

Since so much of our experiences involve others, particularly those who are more than fleeting acquaintances, they are in a sense our co-creators in this life. Unless we are mindful, we may dishonor them by being unkind, by unknowingly creating expectations of them or drawing conclusions about their actions that may not be valid.

Let us take a few moments to talk about honoring the creative partners on our path, especially if they challenge us.

In *The Four Agreements: A Practical Guide to Personal Freedom*, Don Miguel Ruiz said that we create our own suffering because of agreements we have unknowingly made with ourselves. These agreements shape the way we see others and the world around us. They automatically generate back stories in our subconscious mind about what we experience from moment to moment. In turn, these stories guide our decisions and actions.

We are essentially talking about the subconscious programming discussed earlier in this book. For us to awaken to a new dream of a happier, more fulfilling existence, Ruiz urges us to live consciously by four agreements:

- Be impeccable with your word
- Don't take anything personally
- Don't make assumptions
- Always do your best

It is a very accessible book, loaded with great wisdom. I highly recommend that you add this treasure to your reading list, if you have not read this book before.

Meanwhile, let's talk about how the first three agreements are highly relevant to how we honor others. We will talk about the fourth agreement in the *Conclusion* chapter.

First, by being impeccable with our word, we say what we mean, and mean what we say. In other words, we speak from our center of integrity.

When we choose to speak impeccably, we also express kindness, peace and truth. When we choose impeccable speech, we refrain from gossiping, as it is unkind to the subject. If we catch ourselves wanting to say something about someone we would not feel comfortable saying to this person, we are about to gossip.

I like to think of it as someone else's life is not my story to tell. If there is a pearl of wisdom from someone's experience from which others could benefit, I would first ask for permission before relaying the story. Following this agreement does not only honor others, it honors our own integrity. After all, what we say is ultimately a reflection of us, not about whom we speak.

As for the second and third agreements, they can be best summarized as: *Give others the benefit of the doubt.* By vowing not to take anything personally, we choose to recognize that others' actions have nothing to do with us, but with their own inner state.

When someone lashes out at you, that behavior is a result of a wound being triggered within them. Even if they try to make it your fault that you angered them, their behavior is entirely about them, not about you. While the anger directed at you may be hard to take, just realize that it is about the other party, not you.

Have compassion for their inner suffering that produces the behavior, if you feel up to that. But, at the minimum, do not take the lashing out personally. Practicing this awareness minimizes your suffering from others' behavior over which you have no control.

Similarly, with the third agreement, we give others the benefit of the doubt by curtailing our ego's prompting to weave a back story around an event. When other people do not behave the way we expect, or when they say something that surprises us, the knee-jerk reaction is to make assumptions and jump to conclusions about their behavior. After all, we need to make sense of our disappointment.

A better alternative would be to seek clarification. If we manage to do that instead of making assumptions about others' behavior, we cultivate the consciousness for seeing things as they are, not what we perceive or fear them to be. We can save ourselves – and others – from the pain caused by the drama based entirely on our assumptions.

Let me give you an example of giving others the benefit of the doubt. Several years ago, I had just wrapped up a project with a client, and we were working on scheduling a presentation to the leadership team. When I got the draft meeting agenda, my boss's name was listed as the presenter instead of mine. I immediately took it personally, and the back story promptly started forming: *Here we go again, they want my boss presenting the work that I slaved over!*

You see, over the years, I was told explicitly several times that I was too young to be taken seriously. Other times, it was more subtle as to why professional seniority or other demographic factors trumped direct knowledge and experience.

Alice P. Chan, Ph.D.

For instance, one time, after I had just delivered a 30-minute presentation, an elderly member of the audience went up to the podium to ask a question. He looked past me to my boss and said, "*I have a question about what you just said.*" My boss had yet to say a single word. Because of cumulative experiences such as that, I was triggered by the above scheduling situation.

Fortunately, at the time, I was studying *The Four Agreements* intently. So, I caught myself in time before the beginnings of a back story developed into full-blown drama. Upon seeking clarification, the unintentional error of listing my boss as the presenter was corrected. Not only did I end up delivering the presentation, I went on to do two more projects for the same client organization within a year.

What truly touched me was that my contacts there sent me flowers when they heard about my horrific accident at the end of 2008. As clients who paid for my consulting services, they had no reason to ingratiate me. Their expression of caring was purely genuine and heartfelt. I was – and am – truly grateful that I did not let my reflexive personal reactions and assumptions, triggered by old wounds, get the better of me.

The moral of the story is this: When we choose to give others the benefit of the doubt, we save ourselves – and potentially others – from the suffering of unnecessary drama. Ultimately, we may never know the true motivation behind the behavior we see on other's parts – whether there is an innocent explanation or a less than noble intention. In the end, it does not really matter. When we choose to honor others as our default stance, even when it is a challenge, we avoid inviting bad feelings for ourselves and potentially condemning others unjustly.

○ *Contemplation Exercise*

- Think about your latest substantive interaction with someone in your life. Were you impeccable with your word? If not, how may you be mindful of honoring others through what you say or not say? Remember Edwene Gaines' 21-day challenge to rid negativity in your speech from the *Release* chapter? That challenge would be valuable to keeping your word impeccable.

- Think of a time when you felt offended by something someone did or said. Is there a chance that you might have taken it personally when no offense was intended? What in your contemplation led you to this awareness? What would you do to keep up this awareness?

- Think of a time when you jumped to conclusions about what someone said or did. Were your assumptions accurate, or was there another explanation? How would you practice keeping assumptions about others in check?

Remember that we do not want to block our dreams by jamming our creative space with negative energy. When we practice honoring others by being kind and respectful with our words and not engaging in idle gossip, we also honor our own integrity. When we honor others by giving them the benefit of the doubt, we save ourselves from a downward spiral into negativity and tuning our radio receiver to undesirable frequencies. By honoring others and staying in a high vibration, we maintain spaciousness in our creative field for our dreams.

Honor by Surrender

During my recovery from the 2008 accident, I had to accept a period of involuntary surrender. In the first two weeks after I came home from the hospital, I had splitting headaches, and was confined to bed most of the time. I was too weak to do anything, and had no choice but to surrender in every way.

Mentally, aside from some short-term memory loss, I could not think as fast as before, which was truly unnerving. Physically, I could not do most things that I had completely taken for granted. Most of all, it took eight weeks before my dizziness subsided enough for me to feel comfortable driving short distances again.

Emotionally, I had to learn to let others be there for me, including driving me everywhere I needed to go. As independent as I was, it made me feel very vulnerable to need others.

The whole experience was very humbling, and it gave me a true taste of what it was like to be in total surrender mode. Spiritually, I knew this trauma was meant to serve a purpose, and I spent a lot of my time at rest in meditation and contemplation.

Ultimately, as you read in the *Release* chapter, the accident came as a result of avoiding my inner call to step into my Zone of Genius – to develop REACH and spread the message. Beyond that, the trauma taught me to honor the wisdom of giving up control – and surrender.

Even though surrendering control takes practice, it is absolutely for our highest good. Control is ultimately a fear-based need. It imprisons us in our own suffering, when we get ourselves all wound up around expectations of how others need to behave. We need things to go our way, lest our world crumbles.

And, yet, when we give up control – voluntarily or not – the world around us still stands. What fall apart instead are our illusions of safety, the walls we have built up around ourselves to hide our vulnerabilities, to control our environment, to keep ourselves safe.

Surrender ultimately builds faith, because we get to witness first-hand how people and things – without our direction or control – line up on their own to support and help us. When we surrender, we get out of our own way and allow things to happen according to their own will. The results are often far better than what we can orchestrate ourselves.

When you surrender control of your dream, you honor it by allowing cosmic wisdom to work its magic on your behalf. Take care of what is yours to do, and surrender control of the rest. That is, do your releasing, envisioning, taking guided action, celebrating and honoring yourself and where you are on your path. But, when it comes to *how* precisely your dream should unfold, have faith in the conscious work you have done to realize your dream.

If you have done your due diligence with REACH – not just going through the motion – as we have covered a few times already, it is by universal law that the external circumstances of your life must line up to match your internal state.

In my last attempt to write this book, I get to experience the sweetness of surrender. After the previous aborted attempts at writing, I am finally in the right place to surrender control.

When I sit down to write, I allow myself to be guided by my inner creativity that is connected to source energy. As a result, this book has been written out of sequence. The first substantive chapter I was inspired to write after the *Prologue* and *Introduction* was actually this chapter on *Honor*. I am just now coming back to complete what was started two months ago. *Celebrate* came after *Envision*, and *Act* was the last substantive chapter I wrote in full.

The creative process has been completely organic, unlike the sequential, structured one I used for academic and business writing. Yes, I still have an outline and basic structure to the book. And, yes, I do have a SMART plan for getting this book written on a timely basis. But, when I feel inspired to write something on a different chapter than the one I am currently working on, I follow it.

By not forcing my writing to conform to a rigid plan, I allow a deeper and richer book to emerge. By surrendering to what needs to be written and when, my last attempt at writing this book has been a truly exquisite experience.

Surrendering attachment to the specifics of how your dream plays out can be the best thing for its realization. Be willing to consciously detach from your need to control the details of the manifestation process. Doing so opens up space for something potentially much better for your dream. (Spoiler alert: A lot of those details are out of your control anyway!)

If you feel any tension from trying to do things in a certain way – even if you had recurring success with it in the past – notice that tension. It may be telling you that this process or method no longer serves you. Honor the purpose it once served, and let it go. Surrender to the present and what better suits the evolved you.

O *Contemplation Exercise*

- Think of a time when you believed that if you did not take control of a situation, things would either not happen or would fall apart. What were the circumstances?
- For now, allow the possibility that the situation would have turned out just fine without your control. Without thinking too hard, start writing what you think could have happened. For example:
    - Who might have stepped in to handle the situation?
    - What alternative chain of events might have transpired?
    - What might have been the outcome?
- Don't slip into take-charge, problem-solving mode. Instead, just allow your stream of consciousness to come to you.

What did you learn from this contemplation? Do you see that things have a way of working themselves out without your intervention? By consciously choosing to surrender, you not only ease yourself from the burden of having to be the responsible one all the time. You also allow others to be of service and shine. It is true that the outcomes may be different from what you might expect. But, sometimes, they are even better than you would want.

Now that we are at the end of this last pillar of REACH, *Honor*, I can basically sum this chapter up with a simple message to you: *You're ok!*

It is commendable that you have the desire to improve yourself and/or your life for the sake of growth and evolution. But, remember that what you do or not does not fundamentally affect your self-worth or lovability. Moreover, even if you feel lost and do not know what you want, trust that you are just in the outer folds of the labyrinth of life.

By the same token, while some things are challenging to honor at their face value – the waiting time for your dream to manifest, distractions and challenging people on your path – trust that they are valid parts of the labyrinth of life. If you just keep the faith, pay attention to the intuitive intelligence coming through your body, do your part and surrender control of the rest, you cannot miss your life. If you keep taking one step at a time, your path will lead you to your dream.

Alice P. Chan, Ph.D.

Summary Points for Honor

❖ Honor who you are, with no strings attached. Your self-worth and lovability do not hinge on what you do or not. You are ok just as you are, without any need to be "fixed."

❖ Honor your body beyond taking care of your physical health. Your physical apparatus holds a tremendous amount of intuitive intelligence. It sends you messages for your wellbeing and highest good.

❖ Honor where you are in the labyrinth of life. The seeming detours in your life actually serve to prepare you for where you want to go to realize your dream.

❖ Honor the mystery of timing. The bigger your dream, the more time it will take to manifest. Honor the waiting, as it may also show you that you have outgrown what you thought you wanted.

❖ Honor distractions. They remind you to revisit your priorities and make conscious choices that are right for you. They provide you with the opportunities to choose the route that is aligned with what you really want.

❖ Honor others. Be impeccable with your word, and you honor others and your own integrity. Give others the benefit of the doubt by not taking things personally or making assumptions about others' behavior.

❖ Honor by surrender. Control is ultimately a fear-based need. When you surrender control, you allow people and things to line up to support you – often in ways better than you can orchestrate yourself.

CHAPTER 7

Conclusion

"A journey of a thousand miles begins with a single step."
— Confucius

We have now come to the end of our REACH journey together. What a ride it has been! You have done a lot of great work to get to this point, and I want to congratulate you!

I know that some of the contemplation exercises probably did not feel so good. If you have stuck with me despite that, I know you are truly committed to your dream. Bravo! I hope you have been celebrating your efforts along the way and sending a clear message to your subconscious that you mean business.

Before I wrap up with some final thoughts, let's recap what we have done, shall we?

- We started with some house cleaning in Chapter 2, *Release*, when we used different tools to uncover and let go of some fears and old beliefs blocking our path. In doing so, we created spaciousness in our vibration in preparation for our dream.

- In Chapter 3, *Envision*, we engaged our fearless inner dreamer to imagine what it would feel like to be living our dream. We learned how to allow our inner dream to unfold through meditation, as well as how to get clear on what we want and visualize having these conditions fulfilled.

- In Chapter 4, *Act*, we practiced discerning true inner guidance from ego-based directives, so that we can take guided, inspired action on our dream. We discussed a few simple ways to maintain a regular meditation practice for tuning into our inner guidance. We also started a SMART plan for our dream, which we will continue to update until our dream is fulfilled.

- In Chapter 5, *Celebrate*, we looked at the importance of inviting the energy of celebration into our lives. We began to cultivate an awareness of appreciating and celebrating the good already in our world. We also started making plans to celebrate the progress made toward realizing our dream.

- Last, but not least, in Chapter 6, *Honor*, we looked at honoring the current version of ourselves and where we are in our lives – the here and now from which we create our future. We also learned to honor our body, as well as the mystery of timing, distractions and people on our path to our dreams. We discussed the importance of doing our part and surrendering the need to control the rest.

Continuing Your REACH Practice

As I noted at the beginning of the book, REACH is a roadmap to empower you to become a conscious creator in your life. By now, I hope you have seen firsthand how REACH helps you do that – one moment at a time, one experience at a time. After all, your life is nothing but a series of moments and experiences, some more profound and memorable than others. Once you have developed your "REACH muscles" to create moments and experiences of your choosing, endless dreams and possibilities are yours to behold.

Practicing REACH gradually raises your consciousness, helping you to become increasingly aware of the choices you make – big and small – day in and day out. As you continue to practice REACH, you will likely unveil more latent beliefs and unconscious life patterns. Know that this is perfectly normal, and there is nothing wrong with you or the way you practice REACH.

In fact, speaking from direct experience and others sharing over the years, beliefs are like an onion. Unless you start peeling off a layer, the ones hidden underneath cannot be revealed. Therefore, do not be alarmed or discouraged if you should encounter more hidden beliefs on your path to REACH your dreams. Remember that this is actually a very positive thing. It means you are ready to let go of more blocks on your path. Just use the tools in this book to release what no longer serves you.

Similarly, neither guidance nor action is static. Therefore, aside from updating your SMART plan, check in periodically with your inner wisdom and creativity for updates on guidance. Chances are, as you get more attuned to your inner world, you will notice guidance coming to you effortlessly. But until that happens, when you feel unsure, you can always ask by going into meditation – including the visioning and chakra meditations in the *Envision* chapter – engaging in quiet contemplation and/or doing hot-penning.

The highest and most loving part of you, which is connected to cosmic wisdom, always stands ready to support you and provide you with answers. It is at your beck and call 24 hours a day, 7 days a week. It does not judge you, nor does it get upset at you if you forget about it for extended periods of time. After all, it is the infinite love within you that is unconditional. Just remember that you have a very powerful partner, coach, supporter and champion within you.

As you practice REACH, you will find that it only works if you are *willing* to believe there is a better, easier way to live by raising your consciousness. The alternative is to believe that there is no rhyme or reason for anything, that life is but a big ball of randomness.

If you choose consciousness over randomness, the timeless tools in this book will always be at your disposal to help you manifest your heart's desires. Having said so, my ultimate intention for sharing REACH with you goes beyond helping you manifest your dreams – your current one and others in the future.

It is my genuine wish that you feel confidently tooled up to know how to navigate the labyrinth of your life. It is my most heartfelt desire that practicing REACH helps you build faith in yourself and in life.

One Day at a Time

Please do not set yourself up to fail by being too ambitious or too impatient with the changes you want to make in your life. It is good to stretch yourself in the process of REACHing your dreams. After all, change and growth do require us to step out of our comfort zone.

However, do honor the fine line between stretching and overextending. Provided you approach your REACH practice with good intention and true commitment, cut yourself some slack when things do not progress as well or as quickly as you would hope.

If you are slowed down because more old beliefs come up to be released, know that it is ultimately a good thing. Be patient with yourself if it takes time to get clear on what you want. Forgive yourself if you miss the deadline you set for a SMART goal because of an unexpected distraction. This REACH process is meant to work with where you are in your life, so you get to choose how to pace yourself and adjust the process accordingly to suit you.

If you are new to choosing to live with consciousness over randomness, the change can seem rather daunting all at once. After all, it basically involves an overhaul in the foundational beliefs running your life.

The best advice I can offer you is to take things one day at a time. You are signing up for transformation over time, not a radical shift overnight. It simply cannot be rushed. Take it from someone who was born deficient in the patience gene and over-endowed with the perfection one. You *can* train yourself to be patient and allow lots of room for error – when you either forget to be conscious, or your "consciousness muscle memory" is still in need of strengthening.

When I was new to conscious living several years ago, new to paying attention to how I was unknowingly attracting experiences into my life, it was quite overwhelming. Sometimes, when things were not going well, I found it really difficult to shift my attitude to produce a different experience, even though I knew how it worked. I even said to someone once, *"I just want to be mad for a while! It takes too much energy to be positive when things are just not going my way!"*

Moments like these are bound to come up. If they do, honor that you are *in the process* of empowering yourself, and that you will fall off the wagon every now and again. Forgive yourself, honor yourself, and try again the next day. As you continue to take it one day at a time, it will progressively get easier. In time, paying attention to what you are calling into your life will become second nature to you.

To build your consciousness gradually, choose something specific that you experience on a day-to-day basis. Be really deliberate about the intention you set, the outcome you want, and the thoughts associated with that desired outcome.

To give you an example from several years ago, I was working on a particularly challenging project with a client who was extremely disorganized and did not honor timelines. A project task that should have taken two weeks to accomplish was still not done after two months. It felt like pulling teeth every step of the way, and I was really frustrated.

I decided to shift my attitude and envisioned her being responsive and cooperative. I visualized her emailing me the information I needed and feeling nothing but a sense of ease in my day. When I was done with the visualization, I let it go, and moved onto other projects.

Lo and behold, later in the same day, I got an email from her apologizing for letting things slip through the cracks on her end. This was followed by emails from her and her colleague providing me with exactly what I had been waiting for to move the project along. I did not have to call or email her again, and I got what I needed effortlessly. The best part was that I felt no stress in my day, just as I had envisioned.

My purpose for sharing this example with you is that, when you are new to working with REACH tools, you are just learning to choose your actions consciously. Practice starting your day off setting the tone for how you want it to go. Feel the joy of ease and flow, and then let it go. Know that it is done as you believe.

Your initial successes may be small and may not occur as often as you would like. But let them serve as encouragement to you. It is like exercising muscles you did not know you have. Until you build up muscle tone, the task that engages them will feel effortful. However, as you continue to exercise these muscles, not only will your muscle tone increase, whatever you want to do with the muscles will become easier as well. Practice this consciousness one day at a time.

Always Do Your Best

The fourth agreement from *The Four Agreements* by Don Miguel Ruiz, "Always do your best," is sage advice for us to follow. By vowing to do our best always, even though our best will vary from moment to moment, we avoid self-judgments and regrets.

Doing our best does not mean being perfect all the time. As we discussed in the last chapter, part of honoring ourselves is to embrace our imperfection and the parts of us that are not as easy to love. Instead, our best is subject to fluctuations based on how we feel, and what else requires our attention on a day-to-day basis.

When we know we are doing our best from moment to moment, we are at peace with what did not get done. We honor the effort, and acknowledge without self-criticism what did not get accomplished.

To apply this agreement specifically to REACH, doing our best with each component includes the following:

- Allow the time and space necessary to uncover old beliefs to be released, which often happens in layers. Do not be disappointed with yourself if old beliefs continue to surface when you thought you were done with your release work. Know that this is normal.

- Continue to practice envisioning to allow your inner dream to unfold fully, to visualize yourself in it, and to get clear on what you want. If it takes time to get clarity, honor that, and trust that it will come as you continue your envisioning practice.

- Cultivate your ability to discern and follow true guidance to devise your SMART plan, including anticipating distractions and heading them off. Check in periodically for

- Embrace celebratory energy as often as you can. Choose to live in a state of grace through appreciation and gratitude. Rather than waiting for a reason to celebrate, celebrate the reason into existence.

- Always honor who you are and where you are on your path. Take care of your physical body and tune into its intuitive wisdom. Remember to honor the waiting time for your dream to manifest, distractions along the way and challenging others on your path. Always do what is yours to do and surrender control of the rest.

Always Come Back To Your Mat

Many years ago, a friend of mine shared with me a pearl of wisdom from her yoga teacher. In a very non-judgmental way, the teacher said she would never give anyone a hard time for not maintaining a consistent yoga practice. It did not matter to her how long they had been away from their mats or whatever their reasons were for disrupting their practice. Those were ultimately inconsequential.

All she asked was that they always came back to their mats, that they never gave up permanently on their yoga practice. If they needed to take a break or fell away from their practice for whatever the reason, they should not feel guilty about it. However, she urged them to always return to their mats.

Always come back to your mat. That is great advice, and I am urging you to do the same with your REACH "mat" as well. We are all different, and there is more than one way to reach our dream.

You may find your labyrinth particularly complex to navigate, and there may be more than a few seeming detours or lost moments along the way. What you once thought you really wanted may no longer suit your evolved self in time. Your circumstances may change which, in turn, may inspire different or bigger dreams. While acting on your SMART goals, some hidden old beliefs may surface to be released before you can move on. By getting clearer on your desires, you may decide to change course midstream.

The reasons why you may seemingly walk away from your dream are countless. But always trust this one thing: As you embark on your REACH journey, you will get more tuned into where you are in your labyrinth, and what is best for you at any given moment. Honor that, and trust that you will always find your way back to what you need to do.

As long as you keep saying "Yes" to that inner voice, feeling, vision or knowing calling you, you cannot miss your life. Your life – and, more importantly, you – are so important to the universe that you simply cannot be lost forever. All you have to do is be *willing* to come back to your mat always, no matter how long you have been away and for whatever the reason.

In closing, I am beyond thrilled and incredibly humbled all at the same time. As I write these closing remarks, the completion of this project fulfills a long-time dream – to have this book published and in your hands.

The dream of this book is part of a bigger dream – to fulfill my life purpose by being of service. I feel such a tremendous honor and privilege to be the messenger of REACH as expressed through my voice, framed through the lenses of my life experiences.

Moreover, on most writing days like today, I get to experience the exquisiteness of falling in love with life over and over again. In convey-

Alice P. Chan, Ph.D.

ing the message of REACH, I get to choose again and again to live in a state of grace, to soar with the beauty and joy of living this charmed life, to savor how truly blessed I am.

Thank you so much for this great honor and privilege to be your guide to *REACH Your Dreams*!

EPILOGUE

I originally wrote this section as part of the *Act* chapter. After all, it is all about the different ways that guidance comes to us. However, as I continued to write, I felt that the chapter was already getting dense. It is a lot of information to digest, especially if you are new to this type of content. So, I asked myself how critical it is for you to know the information below for the purpose of letting your inner dream unfold.

I decided that it is nice to have, but not critical, at this point. So long as you practice meditation regularly, you will receive the insights you need to unfold your inner dream and to be guided to take appropriate action.

What's more, as you build up your meditation practice, your connection with your inner wisdom will strengthen, and you will become aware of your natural intuitive abilities – if you aren't already – even if you may not know immediately what they are.

So, I will leave it up to you on how much you choose to assimilate what is shared below. If you have already experienced some of these insights without knowing what they were, now you have reference points.

Whether or not you already have direct experience, know that practicing your ability to recognize different types of intuition and synchronicities can strengthen your connection to cosmic wisdom. However, if I were to prioritize where you spend your energy for the sake of REACHing your dreams, I would focus on the tools and practices in the main chapters.

Keep this *Epilogue* as a reference. If and when you want to practice tuning into these sources of guidance, this material will always be here.

Cosmic wisdom comes to us through a number of different avenues, including what is known as *intuition*. Intuition involves having insights without conscious thought or a reasoning process. Since it is not logic-based, many of us are skeptical of such ability. Yet, when we learn to trust this wisdom and follow its guidance, we can break through the limits of our rational mind. By tuning into this wisdom, we can see beyond what our risk-adverse ego would like us to see.

Before we proceed further, some of you may not be ready to embrace the concept of intuition, and the coming pages may be too esoteric for your taste. If this describes you right now, try suspending your disbelief temporarily. Read this *Epilogue* with an open mind.

For what it is worth, I am a rigorously trained quantitative social scientist, who greatly values logical analysis and knowledge based on objective evidence. However, I also know that rationality has its limits, and it cannot explain fully the awesome mystery of life in the universe.

Therefore, it is for our own good to be open to receiving this great gift of unexplainable insight we all have called intuition. Before you potentially *choose* to do without something, at least allow yourself the opportunity to be introduced to it. Know that, if after you read the following, you still cannot embrace intuition, you have the free will to ignore it.

Four Types of "Clair"

Our intuition comes in one or more of the following four forms: *clairvoyangce, clairaudience, clairsentience and claircognizance*. The French root, "clair" means clarity. Therefore, the labels for the four types of intuition mean clarity through seeing, hearing, feeling and knowing, respectively.

With all four types of intuition, we do not know how we get an insight, nor can we explain it; it is not a product of our rational mind. Whether we are aware, we have access to all four types of intuitive clarity. It simply takes practice to notice and develop these abilities.

Some of us may find it easier and more natural to tune into one or two types of "clair" than the rest. Below is a brief description of each.

- *Clairvoyance* is the ability to see images of the insights our higher self wants us to know. These visual insights are often about the future or the real truth behind a situation that eludes the physical eye. Remember the Third Eye Chakra introduced in the *Envision* chapter? This is the energy center associated with clairvoyance. People with highly developed clairvoyance can see into the future easily, even without getting into a meditative state.

- *Clairaudience* is the ability to hear messages, often without sound. These messages are from our inner wisdom that may include, but are not limited to, something about the future, answers to a real-time question, and warnings about a situation. There are two Ear Chakras in between our Throat and Third Eye Chakras that are associated with clairaudience. People who are highly clairaudient hear guidance all the time.

- *Clairsentience* is our intuition communicating to us through feelings and physical sensations. Our Heart Chakra is the primary energy center associated with this form of intuitive intelligence. However, clairsentient sensations can show up in any other parts of our body. Clairsentient people feel the truth about themselves, others and situations

- whether or not they have already occurred – without knowing why. They easily receive wisdom and guidance through different feelings in their bodies.

- *Claircognizance* is a sense of knowing something without understanding why we know it; we just do. Again, this knowing can be of ourselves, others and/or events that have yet to transpire. Our Crown Chakra, which is connected to cosmic wisdom, is our chief energetic conduit for this form of intuition. Those who are highly claircognizant simply know what in a situation is best for all involved.

Some of you may have already experienced one or more of the above types of intuition without knowing why or what it is. Even if you have not, know that greater wisdom and guidance beyond the confines of your rational mind are available to you. You just need to believe and pay attention.

For me, I mostly get clairaudient insights. They come most easily when I meditate, but I do not have to be in a meditative state to hear insights I need to hear. I have also heard answers to questions posed to a few people with whom I am especially connected energetically – without actually talking with them aloud.

Aside from clairaudience, I sometimes see clairvoyant images about the future when I meditate, such as when doing the visioning and chakra meditations. I would get still images or moving pictures – as if watching a movie in my mind's eye – usually involving locations and sometimes people I have never seen before in my life. Through these intuitive pictures, I get to experience a tiny slice of my future life.

Meditation is the best way to develop our intuition and access guidance when we have a question. However, being in a meditative state is by no means the only time we receive intuitive guidance. When we are really tuned in and have little resistance, our intuition is always "on." In critical situations, our inner wisdom will get our attention through our body or one of the four types of "clair." As a case in point, I have a very special example of an unexpected experience with clairsentience and claircognizance.

It was 1997, two days before my interview at Cornell University for a faculty opening. Academic interviews are typically intense events that last two days, with the job candidate being passed from one individual or group to another from breakfast through dinner.

For major research universities, like Cornell, the most critical element that could make or break a candidate's chances is his/her research presentation, proverbially known as the "job talk." The job talk is usually based on empirical research the candidate has conducted. It gives the hiring university a chance to see what kind of a researcher this person is and what kind of subject matter expertise s/he contributes to the field. Most importantly, it answers the question of whether this candidate has the track record or the aptitude to be a leader in the field, depending on the seniority of the appointment.

Anyway, two days before my big interview, I had a dry run of my job talk with the professors in the department where I was getting my doctorate. I had no previous experience interviewing for academic positions, so I thought it was a good idea.

To my great despair, by the end of the talk, the group had me convinced that I would go to Ithaca and fall flat on my face! The conference room barely cleared before I completely fell apart. I went home that day completely shaken to my core, scrambling hard in my mind on how I could graciously bow out of going to this interview. How could I avoid humiliating myself and my school?

In the midst of being gripped by this fear, all of a sudden, a great calmness descended upon my body and soon filled up my entire being. Without knowing why or how, my intense fear was instantly replaced by an unexplainable certainty that the interview would go very well. The deflating comments I heard in the conference room earlier in the day did not hold any more charge. Instead, I felt perfectly confident and prepared for this interview of a lifetime. All would be well.

I ended up getting the job. And, in case you are curious, my job talk went over famously. My inner wisdom knew what my fearful ego did not know, that being a Cornell faculty member was meant to be a part of my life path.

This intuitive knowledge revealed itself in a very dramatic way that I could not miss. What's more, my clairsentience and claircognizance delivered to me exactly what I needed at the time: The calmness and confidence to be myself and to do what I had planned to do. The action defied what my rational mind and fearful ego wanted me to do instead, i.e., find a way to get out of going to the interview, since I was going to fail.

Dreams

In 2005, I was in a job that did not turn out to be what I had hoped. In addition, I felt really tortured that I did not know my life purpose, and could not fulfill it professionally. So, I felt the desire to leave that job to explore other possibilities, including potentially going back to school to get a counseling degree.

As you might expect, the idea of leaving my livelihood was scary, and I truly wondered if I would be able to land on my feet unscathed. The answer to my question came in a very vivid dream.

In the dream, I was walking up a windy, rusty ramp dragging along a roller-board carryon. The ramp was fairly steep, leading up to somewhere I could not see. As soon as I walked past a section, the rust caved, and that part of the ramp was gone. So, turning back was not an option. As I went higher, I got more scared. Finally, the ramp led to a dead stop, and I was standing in a platform floating mid-air.

REACH Your Dreams

Far off into the distance ahead and many stories below where I was standing, there were two platforms. Either looked too far to reach in a single leap, but I saw no other option. I had to jump. I knew I could not do that with my baggage in tow. So, I dropped the carryon suitcase, and heard a loud thump when it hit the ground below.

Then, I gathered up all the courage I could summon and leapt. As my feet left the platform, I felt something literally hanging onto my back, as if a spring was attached to it. As a result, my leap turned out to be a very slow, controlled jump, instead of the free fall I dreaded. (I hate the feeling of free falling. That is why I would not go near a rollercoaster.) I landed perfectly on one of the platforms that looked impossible to reach a short moment ago. I landed on my feet unscathed.

I probably do not even need to explain my dream; the symbolism is very obvious. No turning back but only ahead, going up a rusty path? My baggage being a liability I had to drop before making a seemingly impossible leap? My leap of faith being a controlled jump that got me on safe ground, without being hurt and not nearly as scary as I had feared?

This whole dream was my intuition telling me that leaving my job to explore my options was the only way ahead. There was no regressing in life and no turning back for sure. However, I first had to drop any emotional baggage – fears and trepidations – about making the leap and trusting that the universe had my back. I could not have received a clearer, more encouraging answer to my question than this dream.

Dreams are one avenue through which our intuition communicates our truth to us. When we are in deep sleep, our rational mind is shut down.[6] For this reason, our dreams often appear illogical and out of sequence – our rational mind is not available to play referee or to organize the contents of the movie during our slumber. Our intuition

---
6 For a fascinating survey of the functions of dreams across perspectives, from neurophysiology to psychoanalysis, read *The Mind At Night* by Andrea Rock.

is free to talk to us about what is going on in our life that requires attention, including when we have specific questions we are pondering, such as in my case above.

According to Jeremy Taylor, a dream minister and author of *Dream Work*, all dreams, even nightmares, carry messages that are ultimately for our health and wellbeing. For instance, in an earlier chapter, I alluded to recurring nightmares about my unviable second marriage in 2003. The message was jarring, and I woke up in cold sweat night after night for months. Ultimately, though, freeing myself from that marriage was for my highest and best good – and that of my ex-husband as well.

If you tend to remember your dreams, try to keep a dream journal. Even if you only manage to remember parts of a dream, they are still valuable. According to Taylor, even a small fragment of a dream could reveal significant insight.

Note that the people and things in your dreams may not be who/what they are in your waking hours. They serve as dream symbols. For instance, when my mother appears in my dreams, oftentimes, it is not really her, but what she represents. So, when you analyze the meaning of your dreams, try to deconstruct what each element represents – people, things and what is happening. Don't worry about the sequential order of these elements, as this is unimportant.

If you are interested in analyzing your dreams, give the following process a try.[7]

- Record a dream in as much detail as you can recall. You may want to do this as soon as you wake up in the morning, when you are most likely to remember the details of your dream.

- Divide a page into two columns. In the first column, list the people, objects and discrete elements of your dream.

---

[7] This technique comes from Bella Shing.

- With each item listed in the first column, ask yourself what it represents. Don't think too hard. Write down the first answer that comes to you in the second column. Repeat this for all items on your list.

- When you have your interpreted list done, piece together the different parts for the message from your intuition.

Synchronicities

So far, we have talked about intuitive guidance we receive internally. Cosmic insights often come to us from our external environment as well. They appear in the form of synchronicities.

According to the *Merriam-Webster Medical Dictionary*, the term "synchronicity" was coined by Dr. Carl Jung as "the coincidental occurrence of events and especially psychic events (as similar thoughts in widely separated persons or a mental image of an unexpected event before it happens) that seem related but aren't explained by conventional mechanisms of causality."

Put simply, synchronicity occurs when the right thing happens at the right moment without a logical explanation – events that seem to be random coincidences to the casual eye.

Chances are you have experienced some variation of synchronicity, whether or not you were conscious of it. Let's do a quick assessment, shall we? Have you or someone you know experienced any of the following?

- You were thinking about something you wanted or needed, and a picture of it showed up in a magazine you happened to pick up a little later.

- You had a question in your mind about how to do something. While standing in line for your latte, you overheard

- the two people in front of you talking about precisely what you were wondering about.

- You were contemplating whether to take action on something. While driving, a billboard caught your eye – the tagline contained the answer.

- You were troubled by a situation in your life, only to get one or more inspirational email messages encouraging you to embrace the situation, that all would be well in the end.

- You picked up a book, turned to a random page, and started reading a paragraph. Something in the paragraph spoke to what was on your mind, even though the topic of the book was not directly related to what you were thinking.

- You kept seeing the same number sequence (e.g., 222, 627, 777, etc.) seemingly everywhere you went. Even though you did not know what it meant, the repetitiveness caught your attention.

The above are just some examples of synchronicities. Basically, if someone or something magically shows up in your life with timely, useful information, that is synchronicity. When you pay attention, you will notice them everywhere all the time.

These seemingly random coincidences often contain timely and relevant messages to us. In the chapter on *Act*, you read a short paragraph from *Callings*, written by Gregg LeVoy. His writing voice was apparently more head-based earlier in his professional life, having come from a family of scientists and intellectual thinkers.

In his book, he mentioned how he kept finding a Queen playing card everywhere he turned. When he finally was ready to heed the message, he realized that the card was a nudge for him to develop more of his intuition, his feminine energy, to write more from his heart.

I have personally experienced almost all of the above forms of synchronicities, some more than others. In fact, one just happened as I am writing this particular section.

I needed to stop writing to head out for an appointment. As I saved my work, it was raining outside, and the winds picked up. Even though it looked like any other late winter day we typically have in Northern California, I felt a nudge to unplug my laptop. I barely got up from my chair, and there was a power surge! Some 20 minutes later, my mom called, asking if I knew there was a tornado warning where I live. I did not for one second fear for my safety, nor did I truly worry that my computer would have been fried. However, this intuitive hit came just in time for me to provide you with a perfect example of synchronicity!

I also mentioned number sequences in the above list.[8] Over the years, I have received messages through numbers time and again. Just as I wondered about something, seemingly random things like a license plate, a clock or a receipt would show a meaningful number sequence.

For instance, I would often see "222" when I happened to be pondering a troubling situation. That sequence tells me that the situation is being resolved for the good of all involved, and I can just relax.

As another example, I would be thinking of a good idea or holding a positive thought, and "777" would show up. This sequence symbolizing winning has shown up countless times in just the right moment to validate I was on the right thought.

On one particular occasion, as I was taking note of – and feeling grateful for – a particularly juicy, exciting thought about my personal

---

[8] See *Angel Numbers* by Dr. Doreen Virtue and Lynnette Brown. It is a handy little guide to help you decode the meaning of different numbers you see repeatedly.

transformation journey, a taxi seemingly came out of nowhere and sped past me. The number of the company printed on the cab was – are you ready for this? – "777-7777"!

For the purpose of REACHing your dream, synchronicities encourage you to keep allowing your inner dream to unfold. They let you know that your universal manifestation partner is listening and answering your questions, responding to your doubts and fears – 24 hours a day, 7 days a week. However, you must be willing to believe and notice when messages come to you. They may be from seemingly random sources, which are objectively unrelated to your questions or concerns.

Therefore, if you are new to noticing synchronicities, it would be beneficial for you to practice paying attention to them. Start with this simple exercise:

- Think of a question on which you would like guidance. Focus on this question for a couple of minutes.
- In the next 24 hours, pay attention to your environment for potential answers, e.g., signs, license plates, conversations (regardless of whether you are part of them or not), and other communications.
- When you get your answers, note them in your journal or workbook.
- Practice doing this regularly, and record how you get synchronistic guidance.

Play with different questions. See what answers you get and in what form. Over time, you will get a feel for what types of synchronicities really resonate with you.

For me, I am particularly sensitive to number sequences and emails. As you build your practice, noticing synchronicities will

REACH Your Dreams

become a habit, and your inner guidance will direct you to pay attention at the precise moment you are pondering something. Really have fun with this practice!

As you can see, there are many ways we can tap into cosmic wisdom within ourselves and through synchronicities. Our universal life partner stands ready to help us, support us, answer our questions and offer encouragement when we need it. Our job is to quiet our minds to clear the different communication channels – and pay attention.

APPENDIX

My Experience with EFT

I stumbled upon Emotional Freedom Technique (EFT) when I was in search of a cure for chronic eczema on my face I had endured for two years. The skin infection mysteriously started after I came home from the hospital following the 2008 accident, and progressively got worse. Before long, I was living on an extremely restricted diet that was free of dairy, eggs, soy, seafood, beef, nuts, citrus and tropical fruits, garlic, onion, spices of any kind or anything similarly potent. These foods triggered allergic reactions in my body that showed up as itchy, sometimes painful, rashes on my face.

Blood tests showed that I was only mildly allergic to walnuts, pecans and hazelnuts, so my doctor could not tell me why my skin reacted to all these other foods, nor did she have a clue on how to help me. Over time, I sought help from a dermatologist and a couple of Chinese doctors, used steroid creams, took all kinds of herbal medicine that was supposed to treat skin conditions, and had acupuncture treatments. Nothing could cure the eczema.

With little help from doctors, I dove into my own research to find a cure for myself. In the process, I learned that it is common for people who have suffered severe physical trauma or recovered from a serious chronic illness, such as cancer, to have a hypersensitive immune system.

When our immune system becomes hypersensitive, it cannot distinguish between good and bad proteins entering our body through the environment or foods we eat. As a result, normally harmless foods are seen as potential threats to the body, and our immune system proceeds to fight those proteins. That overly sensitive immunity response showed up as skin infection in my case.

When I found an EFT practitioner, she gave me a similar diagnosis to my own research. That is, my body still thought I was in danger after the accident and continued to be in hyper-protective mode. The cure would need to be something that could retrain my body to realize that my safety was no longer threatened, and that it did not need to fight so hard to protect me anymore.

Within a month of doing EFT treatments myself daily, my face noticeably improved. Within two months, I did not even need to do daily treatments. Within three months, I could eat most of the "forbidden foods" again.

About a month into my daily self-treatment, one evening, as I began treating myself, I felt profoundly moved by a deep appreciation for my body. It hit me really powerfully how much trauma my body had endured over the years in order for me to grow spiritually – and how much I had taken it all for granted.

After all, as detailed in *You Can Heal Your Life* by Louise Hay, when our body acts up, something in our life is off-balance and is trying to get our attention. In any event, that profound appreciation for my body marked the turning point to my healing.

It is true that my reason for seeking treatment was to manage the chronic eczema. But, what I got was so much more than relief for the physical condition. Instead of just treating the symptoms, my EFT practitioner helped me look for the root causes of the disease. She guided me to uncover the underlying fears, worries and self-judgments feeding into my body's belief that I was still unsafe, trapped in survival mode.

By gradually releasing those emotional and energetic blockages and stepping into my life purpose – including committing to finishing this book – I trained my subconscious mind into recognizing that I was no longer just acting out of fear to keep myself safe. Instead, I was ready to go full-throttle into thriving mode. EFT ultimately helped me to shift my core beliefs, and complemented my spiritual practice in unblocking my energy channels to allow inner guidance to flow.

One of the best parts about my experience is that it involved predominantly self treatments, even though I opted for three half-hour sessions with the EFT practitioner. She was ready to send me home to do my own EFT treatments after my very first session, because the technique was that easy. I elected to see her two more times because I saw value in having her intuitively guide me in uncovering some deep fears and forgotten old beliefs locked in my subconscious. I greatly appreciated her loving guidance and support.

My experience with chronic eczema shows that physical ailment is ultimately tied to emotional and energetic blockages. That was why medicine was not the answer to the dis-ease. The best it could do was manage the symptoms. Until the sources of blockage are eliminated, the dis-ease persists.

If my experience with EFT resonates with you, I encourage you to look into it more on your own. Seeking guidance from a practitioner in your local area is a great way to let EFT work for you.

BIBLIOGRAPHY

Baker, Dan and Cameron Stauth. *What Happy People Know: How the New Science of Happiness Can Change Your Life for the Better.* New York: St. Martin's Griffin, 2003.

Byrne, Rhonda. The Secret. New York: Atria Books, 2006.

Cameron, Julia. *The Artist's Way: A Spiritual Path to Higher Creativity.* New York: Tarcher, 2002.

Chopra, Deepak. *Power, Freedom and Grace: Living from the Source of Lasting Happiness.* San Rafael: Amber-Allen Publishing, 2006.

Dyer, Wayne. *Excuses Begone! How to Change Lifelong, Self-Defeating Thinking Habits.* Carlsbad: Hay House, Inc., 2009.

Dyer, Wayne. *The Power of Intention: Learning to Co-create Your World Your Way.* Carlsbad: Hay House, Inc., 2004.

Emmons, Robert. *Thanks! How the New Science of Gratitude Can Make Your Happier.* New York: Houghton Mifflin Company, 2007.

Gaines, Edwene. *The Four Spiritual Laws of Prosperity: A Simple Guide to Unlimited Abundance.* Emmaus: Rodale, 2005.

Gottman, John and Nan Silver. *The Seven Principles for Making Marriage Work: A Practical Guide from the Country's Foremost Relationship Expert.* New York: Three Rivers Press, 2000.

Hay, Louise. *Your Can Heal Your Life.* Carlsbad: Hay House, Inc., 1999.

Hendricks, Gay. *The Big Leap: Conquer Your Hidden Fear and Take Life to the Next Level.* New York: HarperOne, 2009.

Hicks, Esther and Jerry. *Ask And It is Given: Learning to Manifest Your Desires.* Carlsbad: Hay House, Inc., 2004.

Hicks, Esther and Jerry. *Money and the Law of Attraction: Learning to Attract Wealth, Health and Happiness.* Carlsbad: Hay House, Inc., 2008.

Hicks, Esther and Jerry. *The Vortex: Where the Law of Attraction Assembles All Cooperative Relationships.* Carlsbad: Hay House, Inc., 2009.

Jansen, Julie. *I Don't Know What I Want, But I Know It's Not This: A Step-by-Step Guide to Finding Gratifying Work.* New York: Penguin, 2010.

Levoy, Gregg. *Callings: Finding and Following An Authentic Life.* New York: Three Rivers Press, 1997.

Lipton, Bruce. "Revealing the Wizard Behind the Curtain: The "New" Biology and Epigenetics." In *Measuring the Immeasurable: The Scientific Case for Spirituality,* 185-200. Boulder: Sounds True, 2008.

Lipton, Bruce. *The Biology of Belief: Unleashing the Power of Consciousness, Matter & Miracles.* Carlsbad: Hay House, Inc., 2008.

Pausch, Randy with Jeffrey Zaslow. *The Last Lecture.* New York: Hyperion, 2008.

Rock, Andrea. *The Mind At Night: The New Science of How and Why We Dream.* New York: Basic Books, 2004.

Ruiz, Don Miguel. *The Four Agreements: A Practical Guide to Personal Freedom.* San Rafael: Amber-Allen Publishing, 1997.

Shimoff, Marci with Carol Kline. *Love for no Reason: 7 Steps to Creating a Life of Unconditional Love.* New York: Free Press, 2010

Taylor, Jeremy. *Dream Work: Techniques for Discovering the Creative Power in Dreams.* Mahwah: Paulist Press, 1983.

Tolle, Eckhart. *A New Earth: Awakening to Your Life's Purpose.* New York: Plume, 2005.

Williamson, Marianne. *A Return to Love: Reflections on the Principles of A Course in Miracles.* New York: HarperPerennial, 1992.

RESOURCES

Emotional Freedom Technique (www.eftuniverse.com)
Feminine Power (www.femininepower.com)
The Tapping Solution (www.thetappingsolution.com)
Totally Unique Things (www.tut.com)

ACKNOWLEDGEMENTS

My most heartfelt *"Thank You!"* goes to my editor, Lydia Harry, for her technical expertise, invaluable insights and gracious gift of love. This book truly would not have been the same without the benefit of her keen eye. Thanks a trillion for helping me reach my dream of completing this book! I also wish to thank Michael Jones for providing some great content feedback as a reviewer. I remain solely responsible for any errors.

I'm greatly indebted to my wonderful spiritual family for nearly three years (2008-2011) at Conscious Living Center (CLC). A special *"Thank You!"* to Rev. Jane Beach for all her inspiring messages and the wonderful classes she had written and facilitated. Because of them, my consciousness had grown, and my relationship with my Beloved had deepened. What's more, I had grown into the author of this book. Without CLC, who knows how much longer I would have been lost in the labyrinth of my life?

I also wish to express gratitude and appreciation for all the great teachers and authors, some of whom were cited in this book, for all that they have taught me over the years. Their wisdom has been a voice in my head, their generosity of spirit in sharing their knowledge and insights an inspiration. I especially wish to thank Bella Shing for being an instrumental teacher in my journey to become the woman I wanted to be. Her guidance also indirectly led me to Conscious Living Center.

A huge round of gratitude and appreciation goes to all my friends who have been there for me in so many different ways. They have supported me through my trials and celebrated my successes with me. I'd like to thank Elena Barrioz for inviting me to Sedona in 2008. Without that visit, I'm not sure this book would exist. I'd also like to thank all who helped me celebrate each finished chapter of this book – Annette Matthies, Adrienne Rush, Diane Endo, Sally Steuer, Anne Williams, Maureen O'Sullivan, Sunny Werning, Christi Lucas and Marilee Clemons. It was great fun and special to have you celebrate with me each milestone for reaching my dream. I'd also like to thank Shelley Motley for her loving support always.

Last, but not least, I wish to include a special note to honor my mother. Mom, thank you for choosing to mother me in this life – and for being my biggest teacher of unconditional love.

CPSIA information can be obtained
at www.ICGtesting.com
Printed in the USA
BVHW041310021222
653299BV00017B/95